AF600158

THE RIGHT OF THE CHURCH TO ACQUIRE TEMPORAL GOODS

THE CATHOLIC UNIVERSITY OF AMERICA
CANON LAW STUDIES
No. 131

THE RIGHT OF THE CHURCH TO ACQUIRE TEMPORAL GOODS

A DISSERTATION

Submitted to the Faculty of Canon Law of the Catholic University of America in Partial Fulfillment of the Requirements for the Degree of Doctor of Canon Law

BY THE

REV. JOHN A. GOODWINE, A.B., S.T.L., J.C.L.
Priest of the Archdiocese of New York

THE CATHOLIC UNIVERSITY OF AMERICA PRESS
WASHINGTON, D. C.
1941

Nihil Obstat:

EDUARDUS G. ROELKER, S.T.D., J.C.D.,

Censor Deputatus.

Washingtonii, D.C., die VI Maii, 1941.

Imprimatur:

✠FRANCISCUS J. SPELLMAN, D.D.,

Archiepiscopus Neo-Eboracensis.

Neo Eboraci, die VI Maii, 1940.

MURRAY & HEISTER, WASHINGTON, D.C.

PRINTED IN THE UNITED STATES OF AMERICA

No. 1–336

PREFACE

Every society of men has need of some form of property to attain the end for which it was established. Out of this need has arisen the right of the Church to acquire temporal goods, a right that is based on natural law as well as on divine positive law. It is the intention of this dissertation to examine the arguments that have been adduced in defense of this right, to evaluate them, and in this manner to construct a solid foundation for the right which is stated simply in Canon 1495, § 1, as "the right to acquire temporal goods, freely and independently of the civil power."

Although much has been written on the property rights of the Church in general, comparatively few authors have attempted to investigate the right to acquire. Even in the works that are available one generally notes a failure to distinguish adequately between the property of the Church and the property of the clergy. Especially has this been true in the development of the argument from divine law. Scriptural texts which refer solely to the right of clerics to decent support and maintenance have been used by many to prove the right of the Church to acquire property. Such texts do not constitute a proof of the Church's right; they have value only as confirming the proof.

As an aid in the construction of a solid argument for the right of the Church to acquire temporal goods an inquiry is made in this dissertation into the arguments that have been brought forth in the past, and an effort has been made to evaluate their usefulness at the present time. The treatment of the Church's right to acquire will therefore be according to the principles of public law. The right to acquire will be studied in its relation to the perfect religious society, rather than in its relation to the members of the society. The object of this study will be the right to acquire which belongs to a perfect society; the right to acquire by taxation of its members, for example, or by other modes of acquisition is not properly the object of a study in public law. The scope of the present study, therefore, will naturally include both the question of the existence of the right, and also the discussion of the independence of the right from the authority of the civil law.

The length of the historical chapter, seemingly out of proportion to its importance, is due in part to the distinctly discursive nature of historical exposition, and in part to the author's desire to make his investigation of the Church's right to acquire as complete as possible with the facilities for research at his disposal.

The author wishes to express his sincere gratitude to His Excellency, the Most Reverend Francis J. Spellman, Archbishop of New York, who has made possible for him the pursuit of graduate studies at the Catholic University of America, and to the members of the Faculty of the School of Canon Law for their helpful direction and kind assistance.

TABLE OF CONTENTS

CHAPTER I

PRELIMINARY CHAPTER

Every society of human beings, just as every individual human being, has need of certain material means. A society is an association of human beings grouped together for a definite purpose. The means to be used to attain the purpose of the group will necessarily be proportionate to the nature and the abilities of the members of the group. Hence it is in accordance with the human nature of its members that the society will use material means, *i. e.,* temporal goods, to attain the end for which it was established. In fact it is only by using temporal goods that a society of men can attain its end. These goods may be owned by the society itself, or they may be the personal property of the individual members and dedicated by them for the purposes of the society. But in either case the temporal goods will serve as a means in the prosecution of the end of the society. It would be most difficult, if not impossible, to imagine a society of human beings that could exist and function without the use of material means. If the society is a universal, highly developed society, with many officials, departments, and varied functions the use of temporal means is absolutely imperative. Such a society has a right to acquire temporal goods. Indeed, every legitimately existing society has the right to acquire temporal goods, because such goods are necessary for its maintenance and existence.

The Catholic Church, inasmuch as it is a perfect and supreme society, has the right to acquire temporal goods. This right is an independent right. It comes not from the concession of any human power, but belongs to the Church by right. It is a native right. This has been repeatedly proclaimed by Popes and councils and is authentically stated in the first paragraph of Canon 1495 of the present Code of Canon Law:

> "Ecclesia catholica et Apostolica Sedes nativum ius habent libere et independenter a civili potestate acquirendi . . . bona temporalia ad fines sibi proprios prosequendos."

The Catholic Church and the Apostolic See, in order to claim the right to property, must possess juridical personality, since property is something that belongs exclusively and properly to a person. Canon 100 gives the basis for canon 1495 when it asserts: "Catholica Ecclesia et Apostolica Sedes moralis personae rationem habent ex ipsa ordinatione divina." The Catholic Church as a juridically perfect society[1] possesses personality *ex iure constitutivo,* that is, from natural and divine law, and therefore independently of any positive act of human authority. Since the Church does not derive its personality from another power but exists in its own right, and has its own sphere of activity independently of territorial law, it is to be considered also as a person in international law.[2]

The personality of the Church once established, the right to property follows. Canon 1495 says that the Catholic Church has this right. This is to say the universal Church possesses the right to acquire temporal goods. Temporal goods are actually owned by parishes, dioceses, religious orders, and other moral persons within the Church, and also by the universal Church and the Apostolic See which owns its own goods.[3] The actual owners receive their personality from the universal Church, either by law or by concession of the competent Superior and share in the *ius nativum* of the universal Church.[4] Hence, although actual ownership is held by the individual moral persons within the Church, it is important to establish the right of the universal Church from which ultimately the rights of all ecclesiastical moral persons are derived. Thus, those who, like Friedberg,[5] maintain that the universal Church does not have the right to property manifestly err and endanger the security of the Church's possessions.

The right vindicated by the Church is a native right (*nativum ius*), *i. e.,* a right which flows from the nature and essence of the

[1] Societas iuridice perfecta ea est quae bonum in suo ordine completum tamquam finem habens, ac media omnia ad illud consequendum iure possidens, est in suo ordine sibi sufficiens et independens, id est plene autonoma.—Ottaviani, *Institutiones Iuris Publici Ecclesiastici* (2 vols., Typis Polyglottis Vaticanis, 1935–1936), I, n. 25.

[2] Bettanini, *Il fondamento giuridico della diplomazia pontificia* (Roma, 1908), p. 7.

[3] C. 1499, § 2.

[4] C. 100, § 1.

[5] *Lehrbuch des katholischen und evangelischen Kirchenrechts* (Leipzig, 1903), § 175.

society, and at the same time is in conformity with the intention and will of the founder of the society. Hence, once the Church had been established as a visible perfect society, it was impossible for it not to have the right to acquire temporal goods. In other words, the right to property belongs to the Church by natural law, and (because its founder is divine) also by divine law. Pistocchi has summarized this teaching by describing the right of the Church as "ius non adventitium sed *proprium*, non contingens aut mutabile, sed in suo genere *absolutum* et *permanens,* non ex alterius concessione vel ex simplici devolutione, sed *ex se* ipsa." [6]

The right to property is held by the Church freely and independently of the civil power. The Church, therefore, cannot be coerced in the exercise of its right, nor subjected to the regulations of civil law regarding the acquisition, retention, and administration of property. The origin and the exercise of this right evidence the perfection of the Church as an external and visible society and its superiority by reason of its divine origin.

The right to property is the right to acquire the temporal goods necessary for the prosecution of the ends for which the Church was established. As a human society the Church has need of temporal goods. They are the means it is to use to attain its end. Thus it has the right to acquire them and consequently to retain and administer them. The right to retain acquired property includes the right to possess it and the right not to alienate it except under certain conditions. The right to administer is the right to dispose of property for the legitimate purposes for which the society was established. It is closely connected with the right to acquire and retain.

Although the temporal goods to which the Church has a native right include both *"bona corporalia, tum immobilia tum mobilia"* and *"bona incorporalia"* [7] the present work is concerned exclusively with *"bona corporalia."* Property of this nature obviously includes churches, chapels, cemeteries, benefices, and the lands belonging to them, first fruits, tithes, offerings of money and property (both real and personal), and other revenues. All of these things are destined either immediately or mediately to serve the end of the Church, *viz.*, the worship of God and the eternal salvation of man.

[6] *De Bonis Ecclesiae Temporalibus* (Taurini: Marietti, 1932), p. 7.
[7] C. 1497, § 1.

Church property according to the Code comprises the temporal goods that belong to the universal Church, the Apostolic See, or to any other moral person within the Church.[8] The actual owner of church property in individual cases is the moral person that has legitimately acquired it.[9] It follows, then, that the property of the clergy is not to be considered as church property.

Some of the older canonists distinguished church property into various classes. For example, according to Schmalzgrueber *bona ecclesiastica* were of two kinds: *bona beneficialia,* or the income received by the cleric by reason of his benefice, and *bona mere ecclesiastica,* or the goods that pertained to churches and other pious places, and were to be used for the maintenance of the same, for alms, etc. These ecclesiastical goods were distinguished from the *bona patrimonialia* which were the personal property of the cleric.[10] Reiffenstuel has a similar division.[11] The *bona mere ecclesiastica* of these canonists correspond to the *bona ecclesiastica* of the Code.

From a comparison of the older and the newer concepts it is readily seen that the canonical concept of church property is more clearly defined and more definitely limited in the Code. The present notion of church property includes only the property of ecclesiastical moral persons, and not the property of individual physical persons, even though they are ecclesiastics. It is true that the older canonists distinguished between the patrimony of the clergy and the possessions of the Church, yet the absence of the definite notion that is contained in the present law is, perhaps, responsible for a lack of clarity that is sometimes noted in authors who discuss the right of the Church to acquire property. Saegmueller, to give but one example, establishes the divine right of the Church to acquire and possess property by referring to such texts as Matt., x, 10, and Luke, x, 7, among others.[12] These same texts were used by authors such as Reiffenstuel to establish, not precisely the right of the Church to acquire property, but rather the right of the clergy to acquire decent maintenance and support.[13] Devoti

[8] C. 1497, § 1.

[9] C. 1499, § 2.

[10] *Cf.* Schmalzgrueber, III, tit. 25, nn. 1, 2.

[11] III, tit. 25, n. 1.

[12] *Lehrbuch des katholischen Kirchenrechts* (Freiburg im Breisgau, 1900), § 193.

[13] Reiffenstuel, III, tit. 25, *de peculio clericorum,* n. 7.

admits that church property is that which *belongs to the Church,*[14] yet when establishing the right of the Church to acquire it he refers to the gospel texts just mentioned.[15] Due to this apparent lack of clarity in the notion of church property his argumentation results not in the conclusion that the Church has the right to acquire temporal goods, but in the proposition that clerics have a right to their support.

The present study will adhere to the clear concept of church property as given in the Code. The argument from divine law will show the basis in positive divine law for the right of the Church to acquire property.

[14] *Institutiones Canonicae* (4 vols., Venetiis, 1827), II, tit. XIII, n. 1; tit. XX, n. 1.

[15] *Op. cit.,* II, tit. XIII, n. 2; *cf.* also n. 7.

CHAPTER II

THE ARGUMENT FROM DIVINE LAW

To assert that the Church has a divine right to acquire property is to say that God Himself has endowed the Church with that right. To prove such an assertion it is necessary to show from what God has revealed about Himself that He actually did establish a Church endowed with the right to acquire temporal goods. Hence the argument from divine law is concerned with the evidence offered by Sacred Scripture for the juridical capacity of the Church, and in particular for the right to acquire.

A. The Church as a Perfect Society

The basis of the juridical competence of the Church is the specific character of her social nature. Only insofar as she is a society can she lay claim to juridical personality and the rights that flow therefrom. Thus, in the examination of the Church's right to property, the first thing to determine must be the social nature of the Church. To establish the divine right of the Church to acquire property, it must first be shown that the Church is a divinely established society. Catholic authors agree that if the Church is a society it has the right to acquire property.[1] Hence the status of the Church as a society merits some consideration in the development of the argument from divine law.

An examination of the Church as it is today, as a reality in our contemporary world, will disclose that the Catholic Church exhibits all the elements that are essential to any society. It consists of a multitude of individual members. These individual members are grouped together for a definite purpose. They intend to attain their purpose by the use of common means. Finally, they are directed in the use of their common means by a lawful authority.

[1] Soglia, *Institutiones Iuris Publici Ecclesiastici* (5 ed., Parisiis, no date), II, § 69; Liberatore, *L'Eglise et L'Etat* (Paris, 1877), liv. III, ch. I, pp. 236–238; Moulart, *L'Eglise et L'Etat* (Louvain-Paris, 1895), liv. III, ch. VIII, art. II; Vromant, *De Bonis Ecclesiae Temporalibus* (Louvain: Desbarax, 1927), pp. 1–2; Pistocchi, *De Bonis Ecclesiae Temporalibus*, pp. 5–6; Ottaviani, *Institutiones Iuris Publici Ecclesiastici*, I, n. 199.

These four elements: a multitude of individuals, a purpose, common means, and authority, are the essential elements of a society.[2] No group or union of men can rightly be called or recognized as a society if any of these four elements be lacking. Where they are present, however, they testify to the social nature of the group.

That the Catholic Church has a multitude of individual members needs no proof. Every continent and clime contains men who profess belief in her doctrine and allegiance to her authority. These men are united for a very definite purpose, *viz.,* the salvation of their souls, and the attaining of eternal happiness. In order to attain their purpose they all use the same means: they all profess the same faith; they all use the same means of grace, the sacraments, prayer, the Sacrifice of the Mass; and they all recognize the same authority, the visible head of the Church, the Pope. All the members of the Catholic Church, finally, are united under the same governing authority, that of the Pope, who rules the Church by virtue of a divine commission. Thus the existence of the Church as a society is a fact, an undeniable reality in our contemporary world. Civil governments recognize this fact for they have, and they have had for centuries, their official ambassadors and representatives at the Vatican.

The Catholic Church is not merely a *de facto* society. It is also a *de iure* society. It is because of its *de iure* status that it can claim juridical competence along with and independently of the civil society. For only if it is a legitimate society with the consequent right to exist can it vindicate juridical capacity and the consequent right to acquire property. Since the Church's right to exist comes from the divine will, and since the right to acquire and possess property is a consequence of the right to exist, it is clear that the right to property also is ultimately founded upon the divine will.

The legitimacy of the Church's existence as a society is evidenced by the fact that Christ established it as a religious society

[2] Taparelli, *Saggio Teoretico di Dritto Naturale* (2 vols., Roma, 1855), I, nn. 299–310, 442; Ottaviani, *Institutiones Iuris Publici Ecclesiastici,* I, nn. 15–20. When these elements are present the group is considered a society or an association by the civil law also: "The term (association) has been applied to small as well as to large groups of individuals, but it is usually and most properly applied to many persons acting together through officers or agents in the prosecution of important enterprises."—Wrightington, *The Law of Unincorporated Associations* (Boston, 1916), p. 3.

with a definite form of government. Liberatore calls it the "creation de Jesus-Christ," [3] and both Scheys [4] and De Meester [5] demonstrate that Christ intended to establish His Church as a true society by establishing that Christ Himself positively determined all the elements of the ecclesiastical society.

It is evident that Christ wished to found a society. From among those who followed Him He chose twelve "whom also He named Apostles." [6] These Apostles He sent into the whole world to preach to every creature,[7] to teach all nations so as to make the whole world disciples and followers of Himself: "All power is given to me in heaven and in earth. Going therefore teach ye all nations, baptizing them, . . . teaching them to observe whatsoever I have commanded you." [8] Such, then, was the nature of the society established by Jesus Christ that it stretches out to embrace the whole human race and is not limited by any boundaries of space or time.[9]

This assemblage of His followers was to have a common purpose which was determined by Him in accordance with their nature, and was to be attained by the use of common means, likewise determined and established by Him. For just as He was sent by the Father that "They may have life and may have it more abundantly" and "that the world may be saved by Him," [10] so He too sent His Apostles into the world that all who believed might be saved, and that as many as received Him might be made the sons of God: "As thou hast sent me into the world I also have sent them into the world . . . as the Father hath sent me I also send you." [11] The kingdom which He came on earth to found was not of this world,[12] yet it was to be in this world—an external, visible kingdom

[3] Liberatore, *Droit Public de L'Eglise* (Paris, 1888), n. 234.

[4] *De Iure Ecclesiae Acquirendi et Possidendi Bona Temporalia* (Louvain, 1892), 53–55.

[5] *Juris Canonici et Juris Canonico-civilis Compendium* (4 vols., Brugis: Desclee, 1921–1928), I, nn. 138–139. Hereafter this work will be referred to as *Compendium.*

[6] Luke, vi, 13; Mark, iii, 13; Matthew, x, 1.

[7] Mark, xvi, 15.

[8] Matt., xxviii, 19–20.

[9] *Cf.* Leo XIII, Const., *"Immortale Dei,"—Fontes,* n. 592.

[10] John, x, 10; iii, 17.

[11] John, xvii, 18; xx, 21; *cf.* also Mark, xvi, 16; John, i, 12.

[12] John, xviii, 36.

having an external social organization that was to work for the sanctification of men.[13]

To this end He established and entrusted to His Church the sacraments as the most powerful means of sanctification.[14] He made the external profession of belief in Him a most useful means of salvation[15] and gave commandments which established most salutary relations of charity and mercy among His followers.[16] These were the means to be used by His followers to attain their individual and common end.

Christ provided an authority to direct His followers, the members of His Church, in the use of the means. He established His Church upon Peter and gave him the power to rule and govern.[17] He determined the authority of the rulers of His Church. It belonged to this divinely instituted authority to dispense the means of salvation, to teach men the divinely revealed doctrines of Christ, and to govern the Church with the threefold power essential to every society, *viz.*, legislative, judicial and executive power.[18]

Thus it is shown that Christ Himself positively determined all the essential elements of His society. It is manifest, therefore, that the Church was established by Him as a true society, a society whose claim to existence and juridical personality rests on the most secure of foundations, *viz.*, the divine will. Since, then, Christ established His Church as a society, the right to acquire temporal goods—a right that belongs to every society—comes to the Church from the divine will.[19] Moreover, Christ established His Church as a perfect society. This is clear from the fact that Christ determined as the purpose and end of His Church man's highest possible good in the spiritual order, and endowed His Church with all the means necessary for the attainment of that end. The purpose and end of the Church is by far the noblest and highest possible. It is the supreme purpose; for the Church was established that through it men might attain their ultimate perfection,

[13] Matt., xiii, 3–50; xviii, 16–18.
[14] Matt., xxviii, 19–20; Mark, xvi, 15; John, iii, 5; vi, 54; I Cor., xii, 13.
[15] Matt., x, 32–33; Rom., x, 10.
[16] Matt., xviii, 16; John, xiii, 34.
[17] Matt., xvi, 18–19; John, xxi, 15–17.
[18] Matt., xxviii, 18–20; xviii, 18; x, 40; Luke, x, 16; I Cor., iv, 1.
[19] *Cf.* Tilloy, *Traité de droit canonique* (2 vols., Paris, 1895), I, n. 101.

viz., eternal and complete happiness. That His Church might accomplish this purpose Christ endowed it with all the means necessary.

Although a perfect society possesses everything it needs to attain its end, it is not necessary that the society possess everything actually. Perfection of the society is evidenced not so much by the way in which it possesses the means necessary for its end, but rather by the right to possess them. The perfect society may actually possess everything it needs; or it may possess only some things actually, and others virtually, *i. e.,* it has the right to demand these things of someone, and that one has the duty to supply them.[20]

Actually Christ did endow the Church with all the means necessary for its end, and in so doing He gave the Church the right to acquire property. In order to insure the salvation of men He established a twofold power, the power of orders and the power of jurisdiction. Men cannot be saved without grace. Christ provided the sacraments as channels through which divine grace would flow into the souls of men,[21] and a priesthood to administer the sacraments, the "dispensers of the mysteries of God." [22] Men cannot be saved without knowledge of the truth and proper direction. Christ provided an infallible *magisterium,* sending His Apostles and their successors forth to teach all men, everything He Himself had taught, and promising to be with them, guiding them, guarding them from error all days even to the consummation of the world.[23] To insure freedom from error, He gave special grace to Peter and his successors in the primacy in virtue of which they were to strengthen the faith of their brethren.[24] To direct men in their actions, to promote the practice of virtue, and to prevent men from falling into sinful ways Christ provided His Church with a threefold jurisdiction. He gave it authority to determine the means to be used to attain salvation by making laws, authority to apply its laws, and authority to enforce them with proper sanctions. In other words, He endowed the religious society with legislative, ex-

[20] Ottaviani, *Institutiones Iuris Publici Ecclesiastici,* I, n. 26.

[21] Conc. Trid., Sess. VII, can. 1, 4, 6, 7, 8; Denzinger, *Enchiridion,* nn. 844, 847, 849, 850, 851.

[22] I Cor., iv, 1.

[23] Matt., xxviii, 19–20; Mark, xvi, 15.

[24] Luke, xxii, 31–32.

ecutive, and coactive power.[25] He thus established the Church as a perfect society.[26]

Christ, in giving this twofold power of orders and jurisdiction to His Church, desired that it be exercised by the Church for the benefit of men. The Church has, therefore, every right to use it.[27] Because of its supernatural and spiritual nature only the Church has authority to exercise it and no other society has any right to interfere in its exercise by the Church.[28] But this power cannot be used without the acquisition of temporal goods. It follows, then, that in giving His Church this power Christ gave His Church everything necessary for its efficacious exercise and hence the right to acquire property.

Christ gave His Church the sacraments. The sacraments are sensible signs. Temporal goods are necessary both for constituting and for administering these sacraments. Christ gave His Church a priesthood. But the existence of priests supposes their maintenance. Temporal goods are necessary for this. A priesthood means sacrifice. For the proper celebration of the sacrifice temporal goods are necessary. Christ gave His Church the commission to teach; and, moreover, to teach all nations. His Church was to be a missionary Church, a universal Church. This commission of Christ presupposes the acquisition and possession of temporal goods by the Church. Christ gave His Church jurisdiction—in the external as well as in the internal forum. For the exercise of this jurisdiction temporal goods are necessary.

Thus in establishing His Church as a perfect society, in pro-

[25] Matt., xviii, 19; Pius IX, encycl., *"Quanta cura,"* 8 dec. 1864—*Denz.* n. 1697.

[26] For a more detailed explanation and exegesis of the scriptural texts as well as for a treatise on the nature of the Church as a perfect society see Zapalena, *De Ecclesia Christi* (2 vols., Romae: Apud Aedes Universitatis Gregorianae, 1940), Theses I–VII, XV, XIX; Dieckmann, *De Ecclesia* (2 vols., Friburgi Brisgoviae: Herder & Co., 1925), I, nn. 246–382, II, nn. 642–649; Schultes, *De Ecclesia Catholica* (Parisiis, 1931), pp. 48–49, 257–264; Tarquini, *Iuris Ecclesiastici Publici Institutiones* (4 ed., Romae, 1875), I, 43–45; Cavagnis, *Nozioni di Diritto Publico Naturale ed Ecclesiastico* (Roma, 1886), nn. 302, 303, 309 (this work will hereafter be referred to as *Diritto Publico*); idem, *Institutiones Iuris Publici Ecclesiastici* (3 vols., Romae, 1906), I, nn. 248–258.

[27] *Cf.* Scheys, *De Iure Ecclesiae Acquirendi et Possidendi,* p. 84.

[28] *Cf.* Cavagnis, *Institutiones Iuris Publici Ecclesiastici,* I, nn. 230–231.

viding His Church with everything it needs to attain its end, Christ implicitly established the right, independently of any other society, to acquire property.[29] In consequence of the supernatural and spiritual powers which were to be exercised among men for the benefit of men it has need of temporal goods of various sorts. It needs wine, bread, oil, etc., for the proper administration of the sacraments; altars, churches, sacred vestments, sacred vessels, church ornaments, and many other things for the celebration of sacrifice and the dignified worship of God; it needs houses and material goods wherewith to support its ministers; money and other material resources with which to carry out the commission to teach all nations. It needs tribunals, officials, buildings, and institutions of many kinds for the proper exercise of jurisdiction, and for the fulfilment of Christ's injunction to have charity and mercy towards the poor, the sick, the needy, and the other unfortunate sheep of His fold. In short, for the proper celebration of divine worship, for the support of its ministers, and for the accomplishment of its divinely given mission, the Church of Christ needs, and consequently has the right to acquire, temporal goods—and all this independently of any human power, as will be seen later.[30]

Just as the State would not attain its end or realize its purpose if it lacked the necessary material means, so the Church would not be able to fulfil its mission among men if it had no right to temporal goods. The State needs certain temporal resources for the realization of its own ends, for the maintenance of its officials, ministers, armies; it needs buildings and public institutions. The Church is subject to the same needs. It cannot do without the material resources which are indispensable for the maintenance of divine wor-

[29] Vromant, *De Bonis Ecclesiae Temporalibus,* 1–2; Wernz-Vidal, *Ius Canonicum,* vol. IV (Romae: apud aedes Universitatis Gregorianae, 1935), n. 738; Hirschel, "Das Eigenthum am katholischen Kirchengute"— *AKKR,* XXXIV (1875), 78; De Meester, *Compendium,* n. 1439; Ottaviani, *Institutiones Iuris Publici Ecclesiastici,* I, n. 199; Ferraris, *Bibliotheca,* s. v. "Bona," art. I, 690; Coronata, *Institutiones Iuris Canonici,* vol. II (Taurini: Marietti, 1939), n. 1035; Council of Lyons (1850) can. 23—*Coll. Lac.* IV, 481.

[30] Vromant, *De Bonis Ecclesiae Temporalibus,* 1–2; Scheys, *De Iure Ecclesiae Acquirendi et Possidendi,* 84–85; Hergenroether-Hollweck, *Lehrbuch des katholischen Kirchenrechts* (Freiburg im Breisgau, 1905), n. 1022; Liberatore, *Droit Public de L'Eglise,* n. 234; Soglia, *Institutiones,* II, § 69; De Luise, *De Iure Publico seu Diplomatico Ecclesiae Catholicae* (Neapoli, 1877), tit. 9, p. 31.

ship, ministers, ecclesiastical buildings and institutions. Reason and experience both prove that no religion can exist without the help of material resources, and the Church, though not a religion of the world, is a religion in the world and thus subject to the needs of life in the world.

Since therefore the Church exists, not by human law, but by the positive will of the author of all things, it is also from divine positive law that it draws the capacity to possess everything necessary for its existence and conservation.

B. The Denial of the Divine Right to Acquire

Although from what has been said it is clear that Christ established His Church with the right to acquire property, there have been some who have asserted that Christ forbade the Church and ecclesiastics to possess temporal goods. Epiphanius in his *"Adversus Haereses"* [81] mentions heretics of the second and third centuries who claimed that the Gospels forbade Christians to own property. Arnold of Brescia (circa 1139), the Waldenses, the Albigenses, the Fraticelli, and Wycliffe also asserted that the possession of earthly goods by the Church and by the clergy was contrary to the teaching of Sacred Scripture.

Arnold of Brescia, in an attempt to remedy the evils caused by the bitter conflicts between the bishops and the civil government of Brescia, advocated the appropriation of the property of the clergy. He claimed that all earthly possessions belonged exclusively to the temporal ruler and consequently the Church had no right to acquire; that clerics who owned property, bishops who held royal fiefs, and monks who had possessions were guilty of such grievous violations of the Gospel precepts that they could not possibly be saved; and that all things belonged to the civil ruler, who could not dispose of them except to laymen.[82]

The devotion to the practice of poverty that was characteristic of the Waldenses in the twelfth century seriously affected their views on the use and possession of temporal goods. They regarded

[81] II, 61.

[82] Maroni, *Dizionario,* III, 39, s. v. "Arnaldo da Brescia"; Baronius, *Annales Ecclesiastici* (37 vols., Barri-Ducis, 1864–1883), XVIII, 569–570, nn. 8, 9; Vacandard in *Catholic Encyclopedia,* s. v. "Arnold of Brescia."

poverty almost as the sole means of salvation,[83] and consequently viewed the possession of worldly goods as an obstacle to salvation. Ministers of the Gospel, however, had no right at all to possess property.[84] In this way the doctrine of the Waldenses by attacking the right of the individual cleric indirectly attacked the right of the Church itself to own property.[85]

The Albigenses, by a logical deduction from their fundamental principle that all matter is evil, regarded ownership of property as sinful. The primitive Church, they claimed, jealously guarded the teachings of Christ and scrupulously followed His example of poverty; but by accepting the Donation of Constantine the Church became corrupt. In fact, Pope Sylvester, they said, in accepting the gift violated the precepts of the Divine Master and can justly be called Anti-Christ. They advocated therefore the complete suppression of ecclesiastical property, the ownership of which could not be defended, since it was prohibited by Christ.[86] This is an evident denial of the Church's right to acquire property.

The teaching that Christ and the Apostles owned nothing and consequently the true Church of Christ could not own property was held by the Fraticelli also.[87]

These errors had this in common—they argued that the Catholic Church could not be the true Church of Christ because she owned temporal possessions, and the true Church of Christ had no right to own temporal possessions. These movements were all condemned by the church in local and general councils, but the condemnations were chiefly concerned with their dogmatic teachings.

Wycliffe's theory on ownership was based on the general principle that "Ownership is founded on grace." [88] Now, the concept of ownership (*dominium*) in Wycliffe's day was the feudal concept; that is, ultimate dominium included both possession of the land and complete sovereignty. Such dominium can be said to belong only to God, according to Wycliffe. Therefore, if any creature holds

[83] Tocco, *L'Eresia nel Medio Evo* (Firenze, 1884), 168, note.

[84] Maroni, *Dizionario,* V, 121.

[85] Wernz-Vidal, *Ius Canonicum,* IV, n. 738; *Denz.,* n. 427.

[86] Tocco, *L'Eresia nel Medio Evo,* 84; Poulet, *A History of the Catholic Church* (2 vols., St. Louis: B. Herder Book Co., 1934–1935), I, 500, 502.

[87] *Denz.,* n. 485.

[88] Lingard-Belloc, *A History of England* (11 vols., New York, 1912–1915), III, 308.

property, he holds it of God as the vassal held his fief of his lord. But if the vassal turned traitor to his lord he was not worthy to hold land of him any longer and his land was to be forfeited. Likewise, as long as he did not sin, the creature remained loyal to God, his Creator and Lord. But once he had sinned he became a traitor; for mortal sin is a kind of treason against God. Consequently, he who held property of God could no longer be allowed to do so in the state of sin, and was accordingly to be dispossessed.[39]

Regarding property held by the clergy, he asserted that it was absolutely sinful and unlawful for any monk, friar, or priest to own any kind of landed possessions since they were bound by the words of Christ to lead a life of poverty. It was right, therefore, to deprive clerics of their possessions, and he who allowed them to continue in ownership cooperated in their sin and was himself liable to be damned in hell for thus "soiling the Church of Christ." [40]

Thus Wycliffe opposed ownership by churchmen for two reasons: their personal sins, and their obligation to lead lives of poverty. For either one of these reasons the property that churchmen held could be appropriated. Although ostensibly condemning ownership by churchmen, he really opposed ownership by the Church. Because of the sins of churchmen he claimed that even Church property was lawfully appropriated.[41] His followers, the Lollards, so understood his teachings, and so applied them. "Temporal lords may legitimately and meritoriously take away property from a sinful church;" and again, "If a lord should know that a church is delinquent he is bound under pain of damnation to take away its property." [42]

The scriptural texts which have been alleged by the foregoing heretics against the right of the Church are from the Old as well as from the New Testament. The most important are the following: "The Lord said to Aaron, You shall possess nothing in their land, neither shall you have a portion among them. I am thy portion and inheritance in the midst of the children of Israel. And I have given to the sons of Levi all the tithes of Israel for a posses-

[39] Lingard-Belloc, *A History of England,* III, 308.

[40] *Trialog.,* IV, 18, quoted by Lingard-Belloc, *A History of England,* III, 306, n. 3.

[41] *Denz.,* n. 596.

[42] Baronius, *Annales,* XXVI, 280.

sion, for the ministry wherewith they serve me in the tabernacle of the covenant . . . They shall not possess any other thing, but be content with the oblation or tithes, which I have separated for their uses and necessities." [43]

"The priests and Levites and all that are of the same tribe shall have no part nor inheritance with the rest of Israel, because they shall eat the sacrifices of the Lord and his oblations. And they shall receive nothing else of the possession of their brethren, for the Lord himself is their inheritance, as he hath said to them." [44]

"They shall have no inheritance, I am their inheritance. Neither shall you give them any possession in Israel, for I am their possession." [45]

"Do not possess gold, nor silver, nor money in your purses, nor scrip for your journey, nor two coats, nor shoes, nor a staff." [46]

"So likewise every one of you that doth not renounce all that he possesseth cannot be my disciple." [47]

These texts are regarded as establishing the divine will forbidding possession and ownership of temporal goods by clerics or by the Church.[48]

As far as the Old Testament texts are concerned it will be seen below that the Lord gave the priests and levites the right to offerings, first fruits and cities. The prohibition that the levites should have no part or inheritance with the rest of Israel belonged to the ceremonial or judicial precepts of the Mosaic law which lost its vigor when the Church was founded. Moreover, other texts make it clear that the levites owned property under the Old Law. "The houses of levites which are in cities may always be redeemed. If they be not redeemed, in the jubilee they shall all return to the owners, because the houses of the cities of the levites are for their possessions among the children of Israel. But let not their suburbs be sold, because it is a perpetual possession." [49]

[43] Numb., xviii, 20–24.

[44] Deut., xviii, 1-2.

[45] Ezechiel, xliv, 28.

[46] Matt., x, 9–10.

[47] Luke, xiv, 33.

[48] *Cf.* Carrière, *De Iustitia et Iure* (3 vols., Parisiis, 1839), I, n. 94; Mamachi, *Del Diritto Libero della Chiesa di Acquistare e di Possedere Beni Temporali* (5 vols., 1769–1770), I, 23–144.

[49] Levit., xxv, 32–34.

"Command the children of Israel that they give to the levites out of their possessions cities to dwell in and their suburbs round about, that they may abide in the towns and the suburbs may be for their cattle and beasts." [50]

"And the priests and levites that were in all Israel came to him out of all their seats, leaving their suburbs and their possessions . . ." [51]

"Then the princes of the families of Levi came to Eleazar the priest and to Josue the son of Nun and to the princes . . . and said: The Lord commanded by the hand of Moses, that cities should be given us to dwell in, and their suburbs to feed our cattle. And the children of Israel gave out of their possessions according to the commandment of the Lord, cities and their suburbs." [52]

From this it is clear that the texts quoted by adversaries of church property refer to the arrangement made upon the entrance of the people into Chanaan, according to which the levites did not received a determined portion of territory as did the other tribes, but were given certain cities and fields throughout the land.[53]

If the New Testament texts express the will of Christ that His ministers should own no property, then His own conduct was quite at variance with His teaching. It is well known that Christ and the Apostles possessed a common fund. Moreover, the Apostles to whom were addressed the words under consideration did not understand them in the sense alleged by the opponents of church property. They possessed money,[54] tunics,[55] shoes,[56] and other temporal goods. The precept of Matt., x, 9–10, was merely a temporary one, as Knabenbauer points out.[57] It was intended to guide the Apostles on their first mission when they traveled in familiar country among people already imbued with Christ's doctrine, and preached to those who awaited the coming of the kingdom of God.

[50] Numb., xxxv, 2–3.

[51] II Paralip., xi, 13–14.

[52] Josue, xxi, 1–3.

[53] *Cf.* Hummelauer, *Commentarius in Numeros* (Parisiis, 1899), pp. 372, 373.

[54] Acts, iv, 34–v, 10.

[55] II Tim., iv, 13.

[56] Acts, xii, 8.

[57] *Evangelium secundum S. Matthaeum,* pars prior (Parisiis, 1892), p. 385.

After the descent of the Holy Ghost they were to go to far-off lands, to pagan peoples, and were to preach to those who were hostile to the Jews, or to the followers of Jesus. It is evident that the same precepts could scarcely be given for circumstances so different.

As for the passage from St. Luke (xiv, 33), it would apply equally to all Christians. Christ's meaning was that those who desired to be His disciples ought to be prepared to give up all attachment to their possessions, and even to life itself, should the cause of Christ demand it.[58]

It must not be overlooked that the Church, the divinely appointed custodian and interpreter of the Revealed Word, has never interpreted the texts in question in the sense alleged by the opponents of church property. Instead, the Popes and councils have repeatedly condemned the teaching that it is contrary to the Scriptures for ecclesiastics to own temporal goods, or that the Church had no right to acquire property,[59] and have insisted on the native right of the Church to acquire and own property.[60]

C. Corroborative Argument

1. *The Old Testament*

The Synagogue was the fore-runner of the Church of Christ as the divinely appointed custodian of faith and morals. It may prove useful to consider what were the relations of the Synagogue to temporal goods. Numbers, xviii, 8, establishes the right of the priests to first fruits and "all things that are sanctified by the children of Israel." [61] Upon entering the Promised Land the levites

[58] Knabenbauer, *Evangelium secundum Lucam* (Parisiis, 1896), pp. 438–439.

[59] Martin V, const., *"Inter cunctas,"* 22 febr. 1418—*Fontes,* n. 43; John XXII, const. *"Licet iuxta doctrinam,"*—*Denz.* 495, 500; Council of London (1382)—Harduin VIII, 1891.

[60] Pius IX, *Syllabus Errorum,* n. 26—*Fontes,* n. 543; Choupin, *Valeur des Décisions du Saint Siege* (Paris, 1928), pp. 284–289.

[61] "The Lord said to Aaron: Behold I have given thee charge of my first fruits. All things that are sanctified by the children of Israel, I have delivered to thee and to thy sons for the priestly office by everlasting ordinances."

were not allotted a portion of the land as were the other tribes, but were given cities and fields throughout the whole land in order that the practices of religion might be preserved among all the people.[62] There existed places of worship such as the Temple itself, and synagogues in the cities. Ornaments, sacred vessels, sacred vestments, and other movable goods were used in the divine worship.[63]

It is certain, then, that under the old covenant temporal goods were dedicated to the establishment and maintenance of divine worship. Whether the religious community itself, as such, was the owner of property is not clear. Offerings such as first fruits, for example, certainly became the personal property of the ministers; and the texts clearly establish their right to such property. On the other hand, the ownership of stable property such as the Temple and the synagogues is not clearly defined. It must be remembered that the Jewish people formed a community sacred to the Lord, chiefly concerned with the preservation of His faith and worship. The close connection and harmony between the political and the religious activity of the people assured the security of property dedicated to religious purposes. It never became necessary for the religious leaders to insist upon the right of the religious community to acquire temporal goods. Thus the Old Testament gives no clear and definite indication of the right of the Synagogue, that is, of the Jewish religious community, to temporal goods. However, the texts certainly establish the right of the priests and levites to a certain amount of property.

The fact that temporal goods were dedicated to the ends pursued by the religious society, and that by divine command, is indicative of the divine will regarding the acquisition of property by a divinely established religious society, even though it does not definitely establish the divine right of the society, as a society, to

[62] "The Lord spoke these things to Moses . . . Command the children of Israel that they give to the levites out of their possessions cities to dwell in and their suburbs round about; that they may abide in the towns and the suburbs may be for their cattle and beasts."—Numb., xxxv, 1–3.

"The priests and levites and all that are of the same tribe shall have no part nor inheritance with the rest of Israel, because they shall eat the sacrifices of the Lord and his oblations."—Deut., xviii, 1.

[63] III Kings, vi; II Paralip., iii-iv; Matt., xii, 54; Mark, vi, 2; i, 21; Acts, ii, ix, 20.

acquire such goods. It is in this sense that Fourneret [64] comments upon the texts cited above from Numbers and Deuteronomy. "Or les besoins materiels de l'Église chrétienne, qui fait face, par toute la terre, à des nécessités de tout ordre, ne sont pas moindres que ceux de la synagogue; donc a pari l'Église a le droit de posséder aussi bien que la synagogue."

De Meester [65] and Ottaviani [66] refer likewise to the Pentateuchal ordinances regarding the proper support of the ministers of religion. They use the texts, not to prove the right to acquire, but as an indication of God's will that His Church possess sufficient temporal goods to attain her end.

The texts of Numbers and Deuteronomy refer to the particular conditions of the primitive people of Israel. They contain no reference to the priesthood of the new law or to the Church of Christ. The one sacrifice of the new law is far different from the many sacrifices of the old. Nor are cities of refuge provided in the new law. The provisions of the old law referred to in Numbers, xviii, 8, and xxxv, 1–3, as well as in Deuteronomy, xviii, 1, must be considered abrogated by the establishment of the new covenant.

The texts, however, are not without value. They do show that there was nothing contrary to nature about ownership of property by the clergy; and also that such ownership was not contrary to God's will.

Although they do not demonstrate the right of the Church to acquire and hold property, they do prepare the mind to acknowledge the right of the clergy to acquire property under the new law, and to accept ecclesiastical ownership of temporal goods. The texts also confirm the argument that it is in accordance with God's will for the Church and her ministers to have some portion of this earth's material goods.

2. *The New Testament*

The New Testament texts that are cited in connection with Church property rights may be divided into two groups: 1) those texts that attest the fact that Christ, the Apostles, and the early

[64] Dictionnaire de Théologie Catholique, II (Paris, 1905), s. v. "Biens ecclésiastiques."

[65] *Compendium,* III, n. 1439.

[66] *Institutiones Iuris Publici Ecclesiastici,* I, n. 199, note 14.

Church actually possessed property; and 2) the texts that assert a right to acquire temporal goods. A possible third group embracing the texts that concern the establishment of the Church by Christ has been included in the argument proper.

The first group includes those texts which contain references to the temporal possessions of Christ and the Apostles and to the property of the early Church. Those more frequently cited are Mark, vi, 37: "Let us go and buy bread for two hundred pence . . ."; Luke, ix, 13: "unless perhaps we should go and buy food for all this multitude"; John, iv, 8: "His disciples were gone into the city to buy meats." These texts point to the existence of a fund from which were supplied the needs of Christ and His followers. The existence of such a fund is confirmed in John, xii, 6: "He said this . . . because he was a thief, and having the purse carried the things that were put therein"; and in John, xiii, 29: "Some thought because Judas had the purse that Jesus had said to him: Buy those things which we have need of for the festival day; or that he should give something to the poor."

A similar arrangement was followed by the Apostles after Christ's Ascension into heaven, as is evidenced in the Acts of the Apostles: "All they that believed were together, and had all things common. Their possessions and goods they sold and divided them to all according as every one had need . . . Neither was there anyone needy among them. For as many as were owners of lands or houses sold them and brought the price of the things they sold, and laid it down before the feet of the Apostles. And distribution was made to everyone according as he had need." [67]

To these texts may be added those that recount the collections taken in the Christian communities for the benefit of the needy brethren elsewhere.[68]

All these texts have been used with varying interpretations by the authors. Devoti [69] argues that the Church has always had *bona communia.* Christ, when He established His society, wished it to have common goods, *i. e.,* money collected from the offerings of His followers, and He had a purse from which His needs and those of His Apostles were cared for. The Apostles accordingly were

[67] II, 44–45; IV, 34–35; *cf.* also IV, 36–37; V, 1–10; VI, 1–4.
[68] Acts, xi, 29–30; xii, 25; I Cor., xvi, 1–2; Rom., xv, 26; etc.
[69] *Institutiones Canonicae,* II, tit. 13, ii–iii.

following Christ's example when they made regulations for common property in the early Church. The Church therefore, concludes Devoti, acquired property by the will of Christ and not by virtue of any human law. Sägmüller [70] cites the same texts as evidence of the Church's God-given right to acquire.

Other authors have not gone so far as to maintain that these texts evidence Christ's will that His Church should possess property. They offer the possession of temporal goods by Christ as an example which the Apostles and their successors followed. In this sense the purse of Christ and the Apostolic College can be regarded as the historical origin of ecclesiastical property. The texts, accordingly, afford confirmatory evidence for the argument that the Church has the right to possess and acquire, although they do not definitely establish the right.[71]

Bachofen argues that since works of charity are a necessary part of the purpose of the Church, it must be inferred that the Church, by the will of Christ, has the right to acquire the temporal goods necessary for her charitable activities. Christ commended works of charity to the Church as soon as He had founded it. They pertain to the Church *ratione finis* and if the Church is prevented from performing them an injury is done it. Bachofen cites the following texts: Acts, xi, 29–30: "The disciples, every man according to his ability, purposed to send relief to the brethren who dwelt in Judea. Which also they did, sending it to the ancients by the hands of Barnabas and Saul"; xii, 25: "Barnabas and Saul returned from Jerusalem having fulfilled their ministry"; I Cor., xvi, 1–2: "Now concerning the collections that are made for the saints, as I have given orders to the churches of Galatia, so do ye also. On the first day of the week let every one of you put apart with himself, laying up what it shall well please him; that when I come, the collections be not then to be made"; Rom., xv, 26: "It hath pleased them of Macedonia and Achaia to make a contribution

[70] *Lehrbuch des katholischen Kirchenrechts,* § 191.

[71] Scheys, *De Iure Ecclesiae Acquirendi et Possidendi Bona Temporalia,* pp. 91–95; Satolli, *De Iure Publico Ecclesiastico Disceptationes* (Romae, 1891), p. 134; Ferraris, Bibliotheca (Romae, 1885–1899), s. v. *"Bona,"* art. I, p. 690; Bachofen, *Summa Iuris Ecclesiastici Publici* (Romae, 1910), n. 27; Ottaviani, *Institutiones Iuris Publici Ecclesiastici,* I, n. 199; *cf.* S. Augustine, *In Evangel. Joan.,* Tract. 62, n. 5—*MPL,* xxxv, 1805.

for the poor of the saints that are in Jerusalem"; II Cor., viii–ix, in which the Apostle exhorts the Corinthians to give alms to relieve the suffering and poverty of the faithful in Jerusalem. Since almsgiving and works of charity form so vital a part of the Church's work, it must be inferred that Christ in enjoining upon His Church the performance of such works gave her the right to possess the temporal goods without which charitable work of any kind would be impossible.[72]

The texts that have been thus far considered are evidence only of the fact that Christ and the Apostles possessed temporal goods. Devoti justly asks: "Could the Apostles buy anything unless Christ or they themselves with Christ's consent had received offerings of money?" The Apostles must have possessed money if they thought of buying food for the multitude. St. John bears this out when he observes that Judas had been entrusted with the purse and the things that were put therein.

It is one thing, however, to say that Christ and the Apostles possessed money and temporal goods to satisfy their own needs and to aid the poor, and quite another thing to say that because of this fact the Church founded by Christ has the native right to acquire and hold property. The Gospels certainly leave no doubt that Christ and the Apostles possessed temporal goods, but it does not follow from this that the Church has a right to temporal goods by divine institution. Such a conclusion could follow only if it were certain that Christ and the Apostles possessed their property not merely as private individuals but in their official capacity as superiors and officers of the ecclesiastical society which they had founded. No one of the authors referred to adverts to this point. Commentators on these texts do not refer at all to Christ's ownership of temporal goods.[73] Hirschel, aware of the problem, shows that Christ and the Apostles administered their property for religious and charitable purposes, but does not establish beyond all

[72] *Summa Iuris Ecclesiastici Publici*, n. 27.

[73] *Cf.* Dausch, *Die Drei Aelteren Evangelien* (Bonn: Verlag von Peter Hanstein, 1923), p. 456; Knabenbauer, *Commentarius in Quattuor Evangelia* (4 vols., Parisiis, 1892–1896), *I Evangelium secundum S. Matthaeum*, pars prior, p. 383, 385; *III Evangelium secundum Lucam*, p. 335; LaGrange, *Evangile selon Saint Jean* (Paris: Librairie Victor Lecoffre, 1927), pp. 322, 364; Tillmann, *Das Johannesevangelium* (Bonn: Verlag von Peter Hanstein, 1922), pp. 186–187, 205.

question that they acquired and held it in their capacity as the superiors of the Church.[74]

Likewise the texts adduced from the Acts of the Apostles [75] are evidence that certain property was possessed in common in the early years of Christianity, and from this common fund the needs of the poor were cared for. The faithful sought to imitate the way of life which they knew the Apostles had followed. The wealthier brethren sold their estates and possessions and the money thus realized they divided among the others according as each had need. They did not sell everything they owned,[76] but they sold enough to care for the needy and the poor. Yet whatever property they owned they did not regard as their own but possessed it all in common.[77]

These texts attest a fact. They indicate the manner of acting of the early Church. But to say that they demonstrate Christ's desire that His Church possess property is, at the very least, questionable.

They are not without value, however. They show how necessary the acquisition and possession of temporal goods are for the work of the Church. The quotations from the Acts imply that the early Church was conscious of its right to acquire property; for it is inconceivable that a society that had been founded as a moral guide to lead men to their eternal salvation should illegitimately acquire and possess goods to which it had no right. It is not beyond the realm of possibility, either, that the Apostles were moved by the example of Christ to regulate the common possession of property in the early Church, although there is no direct testimony of this in the Scriptures. Consequently the texts that have been considered in this section have value as confirming the argument that Christ intended His Church to have the right to property, even though they do not demonstrate Christ's will.

The second group of texts contains those texts that assert a right to acquire. The parallel passages of Matthew, x, 10: "The workman is worthy of his meat," and Luke, x, 7: "The laborer is

[74] "Das Eigenthum am katholischen Kirchengute"—*AKKR,* XXXIV (1875), 78–84.

[75] Acts, ii, 44; iv, 32; v, 1–10; vi, 1–4; xi, 29–30; xii, 25.

[76] *Cf.* Acts, iv, 32.

[77] Knabenbauer, *Commentarius in Actus Apostolorum* (Parisiis, 1889), pp. 63–64.

worthy of his hire," and the words of St. Paul to the Corinthians: "Know you not that they who work in the holy place eat the things that are of the holy place; and they that serve the altar partake with the altar? So also the Lord ordained that they who preach the gospel should live by the gospel" [78] are included in this class of texts.

Reiffenstuel [79] quotes the Gospel texts as the basis for the right of the clergy to recompense for their spiritual labors. Hergenroether-Hollweck,[80] Fourneret,[81] and Soglia [82] use the same texts to establish the right of the Apostles and the ministers of the gospel to acquire temporal goods with which to maintain themselves.

Sägmüller, however, would seem to see in these texts the basis of the divine right of the Church itself to acquire property.[83] Liberatore,[84] also, sees in the words of Scripture a basis for the right of the Church itself. His interpretation of I Cor. ix embraces much more than the mere right of the ministers of the Gospel to a decent living. He explains that the servants of the Church "should live by the Church. If this be so, the natural conclusion is that the Lord decided that the Church could possess in order to be able to furnish her ministers the means wherewith they might live. No one gives what he does not have . . . The Apostles affirms as indubitable that 'They who work in the holy place eat the things that are of the holy place, and they that serve the altar partake with the altar.' But if the holy place has nothing, what would you have it give? and if the altar is bare, of what would its ministers partake?"

The phrase used by St. Matthew, "The workman is worthy of his meat," when seen in its context would appear to have no relation to the right of the Church to acquire property. The words are used by Christ as an incentive to His Apostles to go about the work of their first mission with full confidence in God. The Apostles were not to take with them large sums of money, or small change, or even their food, but were to rely on God for everything.

[78] I Cor., ix, 13–14.

[79] III, 25, *de peculio clericorum, 7.*

[80] *Lehrbuch des katholischen Kirchenrechts,* n. 1021.

[81] *Dictionnaire de théologie catholique,* s. v. "Biens Ecclesiastiques."

[82] *Institutiones Iuris Publici Ecclesiastici,* II, § 69.

[83] *Lehrbuch des katholischen Kirchenrechts,* § 193.

[84] *Le Droit Public de L'Eglise,* III, 6, § 2, n. 235.

Since the workman has a right to his food, God will take care that those who work for Him do not lack the necessities of life.[85]

The parallel passage in St. Luke is a little clearer in expressing the right that the Apostles have to receive their support from the faithful. The Apostles were to remain in the house where they were well received, and were not to hesitate to eat and drink such things as would be offered to them; for they had a right to their food since the laborer is worthy of his hire.[86] Unlike St. Matthew, St. Luke emphasizes the right of the Apostles to obtain support from the people to whom they ministered.

St. Luke's words were interpreted by St. Paul as the command of Christ that all His ministers should receive from the faithful the temporal goods necessary for their life and work. In his first epistle to the Corinthians (ix, 1–14) St. Paul, wishing to teach the new converts that sometimes it is expedient to abstain from what is licit in order to obtain some higher good, offers them the example of his own conduct. He points out that since he is a genuine Apostle he has the right to follow the same mode of life as the other Apostles and accordingly to be supported by the communities in which he works. But he has renounced this right, so as not to be an obstacle to the faithful and in order to acquire greater perfection. In the course of this instruction St. Paul asserts that the clergy have the right to be supported by the faithful for whom they labor (verses 4–14). He proves this assertion by the conduct of the other Apostles (vv. 5, 6), by analogies from daily life (v. 7), by the testimony of Scripture (vv. 8–11), by comparison with other teachers and with ministers of the temple (vv. 12, 13), and finally by the precept of the Lord Himself (v. 14). It is in this last verse that he refers to Luke, x, 7: "The Lord ordained that they who preach the gospel should live by the gospel."

In the opinion of Scripture scholars [87] as well as of canon law-

[85] Knabenbauer, *Evangelium secundum S. Matthaeum,* pars prior, p. 383; LaGrange, *Evangile selon Saint-Matthieu,* p. 199; Dausch, *Die Drei Aelteren Evangelien,* pp. 177–178; Meyer, *Critical and Exegetical Handbook,* p. 210.

[86] Knabenbauer, *Evangelium Secundum Lucam,* p. 335; Dausch, *Die Drei Aelteren Evangelien,* p. 456.

[87] Cornely, *Commentarius in S. Pauli Epistolas, II Prior Epistola ad Corinthios* (Parisiis, 1890), pp. 240–251; Knabenbauer, *Commentarius in Quattuor Evangelia, III Evangelium secundum Lucam,* p. 335; Dausch, *Die Drei Aelteren Evangelien,* p. 456.

yers this text clearly establishes *ex iure divino* the right of the clergy to decent support from the people among whom they work. The clergy then have a right to acquire those temporal goods which are necessary for a decent living.[88] To apply the texts to the much more extensive right of the Church to acquire temporal goods would be to extend the words beyond their obviously intended meaning. In an indirect way, however, they may be used as an indication of the Church's right also,[89] for it must not be forgotten that the money and other gifts received by the Apostles were applied to the purposes of the Church. The offerings of the faithful were used to help the needy, to defray the expenses of missionary journeys, and to maintain divine worship.[90]

This indirect method of argumentation, however, has only a corroborative value. It does not decisively establish the right of the Church, but only the right of the clergy.

The divine right of the Church to acquire property is, therefore, not explicitly stated in the New Testament. Consequently, the sole proof of the divine right, as has been mentioned in the first part of this chapter, rests on the fact of the establishment of the Church by Christ as a perfect society. Christ when He established His Church endowed it with everything that was necessary for the attainment of its proper purpose, and hence He endowed it with the right to acquire property. An examination of the nature of the Church as a necessary, spiritual society with a supernatural end confirms this. The arguments offered by numerous synods, local councils, and Popes, and the argument that was to have been proposed by the Vatican Council did not appeal to the New Testament for a direct, explicit proof of the Church's right but based the divine right of the Church to acquire temporal goods upon the divine establishment of the Church as a perfect society.[91]

[88] *Cf.* S. Th. II–II, q. vii, a. 1; S. Augustine in Ps. 146—*MPL,* XXXVII, 1909, f. Satolli, *De Iure Publico Ecclesiastico,* p. 133; Hergenroether-Hollweck, *Lehrbuch,* n. 1021. Cornely points out that some commentators have called attention to the words *de evangelio vivere* which are not the same as *de evangelio ditari.—Prior Epistola ad Corinthios,* p. 251.

[89] *Cf.* Liberatore's argument, *supra,* p. 25.

[90] *Cf.* Hergenroether-Hollweck, *Lehrbuch,* n. 1021; Ottaviani, *Institutiones Iuris Publici Ecclesiastici,* I, n. 199.

[91] *Cf.* Chapter V.

CHAPTER III

THE ARGUMENT FROM NATURAL LAW

BECAUSE the right of the Church to acquire and to retain property is denied by some who reject the fact of revelation and refuse assent to every argument that is not based on reason, Catholic authors have developed the argument from natural law. This method of argumentation, based on the fundamental principles of natural law, prescinds entirely from revelation, demonstrates the right of the Church to acquire and possess property, and shows the proponents of rationalism that even according to their own principles they must logically acknowledge the Church's property rights.

The argument as it has been presented by the various authors labors under either one or the other of two difficulties. Either it proceeds entirely according to human reason and natural law and thus does not present an exact and true conception of the divinely established Church; or it leaves the rational argumentation and builds upon a basis of revelation when it considers the establishment of the Church. In the first case absolute accuracy is temporarily sacrificed for consistency; in the second consistency is sacrificed in order to present a true picture of the Church.

Scheys sensed the difficulty of adhering to the rational method throughout, and elected to base the second part of his argument *ex iure naturae* upon revelation.[1] Moulart,[2] Ottaviani[3] and De Meester[4] were also aware of the problem. They preferred to prescind from revelation and to consider the Church for a time according to the false principles of the rationalists. Ottaviani made sure to remind his readers that although this form of argument proves that the Church does have the right to property even when the Church is falsely considered as a human society, it does

[1] *De iure ecclesiae acquirendi et possidendi bona temporalia,* pp. 51–75. In the very beginning of this argument he remarks: "Quum ecclesia in hac perfectissima forma quam a Christo accepit sit institutio plane positiva, argumentum utique non est ex iure naturali quoad hanc partem qua affirmatur Ecclesiam Christi veram esse societatem, ipsamque solam iam nunc constituere societatem religiosam publicam."—p. 1, note 1.

[2] *L'Eglise et L'Etat,* liv. III, ch. VIII, art. I.

[3] *Institutiones Iuris Publici Ecclesiastici,* I, n. 198.

[4] *Compendium,* n. 1439.

not prove the Church's complete independence and freedom from the civil power.[5] This method of argumentation has several advantages over the other method. It developes entirely according to reason and natural law, and does not shift its emphasis from reason to revelation. It proceeds from premises which are more readily acknowledged by modern jurists. It obviates the necessity of demonstrating the existence of the supernatural as an essential prerequisite to the establishment of the right to acquire property. Its most serious disadvantage, however, is that it assumes an entirely false concept of the nature and constitution of the Church. In spite of this deficiency this method would seem to be preferred when there is question of controversy with contemporary jurists who not only prescind from but actually deny the existence of the supernatural.[6]

The argument from natural law establishes the legitimacy of the Church's right to property. It has therefore a real, although a relative, value. In a society that recognizes only the rights of man—to the exclusion of all other rights—it vindicates the Church's rights according to the common law of religious societies. Thus it is forced to present an arbitrary and false concept of the nature and constitution of the Church, a concept which is held by those modern governments that profess religious neutrality. The notion of the Church that emerges from this mode of argument is that of a human society originating in the wills of its members and drawing from them its rights.

Nevertheless, the conclusion reached is the same as that of the argument based on revelation. The latter argument may be ad-

[5] "Hoc argumento non resultat quidem Ecclesiae ius liberum et independens esse a civili potestate: quia de Ecclesia nunc agimus utendo criteriis pure naturalibus, ut argumentum efficax sit etiam coram illis atheis qui saltem admittunt ecclesiam esse societatem honestam et utilem bono publico." —*Institutiones*, I, n. 198, note 2.

[6] In the United States the Catholic Church is not recognized as a public society. Individual church corporations are regarded as voluntary associations and have no higher status than other organizations formed by citizens. "Religious organizations come before the courts in the same attitude as other voluntary associations for benevolent or charitable purposes, and their rights of property or of contract are equally under the protection of the law, and the action of their members subject to its restraint."—Zollman, American Church Law (St. Paul: West Publishing Co., 1933), § 126; *cf.* Watson v. Jones, (1871), 80 U. S. (13 Wallace) 679.

dressed to those of the faith. The argument from natural law will carry weight with those outside the Church whose abilities are restricted to the limitations of pure reason.

A. The Right of a Society to Property

The right of a society to acquire property is based on its right to existence. If a society has the right to exist, it has also the right to acquire property. The society's right to exist is nothing else but the right of individual men to associate together to form a society. The right to form societies is natural to man, for man has the right to seek the company of his fellows in order to attain with their help some legitimate end which surpasses the strength of the individual alone. The society so formed has the right to pursue its end unmolested as long as it does not interfere with any higher society.

The right to form associations or societies whose purpose is legitimate and whose means are honest flows from individual liberty and from the necessities of human nature. It is a natural right.[7] This maxim cannot reasonably be questioned. The individual experiences within himself certain needs which he, as an individual, is incapable of satisfying. Lest nature be guilty of implanting within man needs and desires which cannot licitly be satisfied, the individual must have the right to unite with other men to satisfy the needs he feels. In this way he is able to attain by common effort those things which cannot be achieved by individual endeavor. To enter into a society of this kind is, therefore, natural to man.[8]

What these necessities are that compel the individual to form

[7] Moulart, *L'Eglise et L'Etat,* liv. III, ch. VIII, art. I; Cavagnis, *Institutiones Iuris Publici Ecclesiastici,* III, n. 382; Taparelli, *Saggio Teoretico di Dritto Naturale,* II, n. 1471.

[8] *Cf.* Leo XIII, encycl. *"Rerum Novarum,"* 15 maii 1891: "Particular societies, although they exist within the State, nevertheless cannot be prohibited by the State, absolutely and as such. For to enter into a society of this kind is the natural right of man; and the State must protect natural rights, not destroy them; and if it forbids its citizens to form associations it contradicts the very principle of its own existence; for they and it exist in virtue of the same principle, *viz.,* the natural propensity of man to live in society."—translation from *Four Great Encyclicals* (New York: Paulist Press, 1931), 28–29.

societies, and how far they induce man to live his life in company with his fellows will have to be determined by a study of the individual societies into which he has entered. St. Thomas, however, has described how greatly man of his very nature needs the help of other men.

> It is natural for man to be a social and political animal, to live in a group, even more so than all other animals, as the very needs of his nature indicate. For all other animals nature has prepared food, hair as a covering, teeth, horns, claws as means of defence, or at least speed in flight. Man, on the other hand, was created without any natural provision for these things. But, instead of them all he was endowed with reason, by the use of which he could procure all these things for himself by the work of his hands. But one man alone is not able to procure them all for himself; for one man could not sufficiently provide for life, unassisted. It is, therefore, natural that man should live in company with his fellows.
>
> Moreover, all other animals are able to discern by inborn skill what is useful and what is injurious; just as the sheep naturally regards the wolf as his enemy. Some animals even recognize by natural instinct certain medicinal herbs and other things necessary for their life. Man, however, has a natural knowledge of the things which are essential for his life only in a general fashion, inasmuch as he has power of attaining knowledge of the particular things necessary for human life by reasoning from universal principles. But it is not possible for one man to arrive at a knowledge of all these things by his own individual reason. It is, therefore, necessary for man to live in a group so that each one may assist his fellows, and different men may be occupied in seeking by their reason to make different discoveries, one, for example, in medicine, one in this and another in that.
>
> This point is, further, most plainly evidenced by the fact that the use of speech is a prerogative proper to man. By this means one man is able fully to express his conceptions to others. Other animals, it is true, express their feelings to one another in a general way, as a dog may express anger by barking and other animals may give vent to their feelings in various manners. So man communicates with his kind more completely than any other animal known to be gregarious.[9]

The freedom to associate with others for some legitimate purpose is, then, natural to man. But not every association of

[9] *De Regimine Principum* I, 1—translated into English by Gerald B. Phelan, Ph. D., and published under the title *On the Governance of Rulers* by Sheed and Ward, New York, 1938.

individuals is a society, unless there exist some moral bond which would make a unit of the many individuals. This bond makes a united body, a living organism. Without it the members would be only isolated individual persons. With it they form a society with rights, collective interests and social needs. This moral bond which is so important arises from the nature of things. It can subsist without legal fiction, without the assistance of the civil authority. Else, how explain the civil society itself? This moral bond gives the society its personality. Its juridical personality or juridical capacity follows necessarily and with it the right to acquire property. Thus societies formed as a result of the impulses of human nature possess juridical personality and the right to acquire and retain property—and all this independently of the civil law.[10]

It has been objected that although the right to associate comes from nature, the right to acquire property is given to the society not by nature but only by the civil law.[11] Such a view is based on the false supposition that juridical personality can be granted only by the civil law. It fails to consider that every legitimate association is naturally a *subiectum iuris*. There are rights that belong to a legitimate society by the very fact that it is a society. The right to property is one of these. It may derive from the nature of the society or from the physical persons who compose it and who can communicate to it their natural right to acquire property. In either case the source of the right is superior to the civil law. If this be not admitted it is impossible to justify the right of the civil power itself to possess.[12]

This does not necessarily mean that the society is entirely independent of the civil power. Within the State the civil authorities exercise control over all imperfect societies in the political order. Yet it is maintained that not all the rights of inferior societies spring from the civil law; and that if a society possesses

[10] Ottaviani, *Institutiones Iuris Publici Ecclesiastici,* I, n. 27, pp. 67–68; Moulart, *L'Eglise et L'Etat,* liv. III, ch. VIII, art. I, p. 552; *cf.* also Bonfante, *Istituzioni di Diritto Romano* (Roma: Istituto di Diritto Romano, 1934), § 19, p. 66.

[11] *Cf.* Caterbini, *Il Diritto Ecclesiastico Italiano,* n. 143; Ottaviani, *Institutiones Iuris Publici Ecclesiastici,* I, n. 198.

[12] Cavagnis, *Institutiones Iuris Publici.* III, n. 369; Moulart, *L'Eglise et L'Etat,* liv. III, ch. VIII, art. I.

independently of the law the right to exist, it possesses also the right to acquire property in order to maintain its existence. Freedom to form societies would be illusory without the correlative freedom of the society to acquire and possess temporal goods. The right to exist gives to the individual the right to acquire those things necessary for his life and the purpose of his life. It is the same with legitimately formed societies. Would it not be absurd for nature itself to recognize man's right to form societies, if the societies once formed were to be condemned to perish for want of the power to satisfy the needs and wants which arise as a result of their creation? Among the needs of the societies one of the more pressing is that of acquiring and having temporal goods.

B. The Religious Society

Religion, viewed historically, has always taken the form of an association. The worship of the Supreme Being has always been a social act. This is not to deny that individual persons have worshiped in private. The point that is important is that even though men have given expression to their religious sentiment in private, the principal expression of religion has been social worship. The religious society is the traditional outward expression of the tendencies of human nature.

It need hardly be pointed out that the Catholic Church is a religious organization or society, whose purpose is the worship of God and the spiritual welfare of men. That is a fact recognized even by non-Catholics. The purpose of the Church is certainly not an illicit or illegitimate one. On the contrary, it is in accordance with nature, since man is bound by nature to recognize and acknowledge his relation to the Divinity. A religious organization that helps man fulfill this duty certainly has a right to exist, and every man has the right to associate himself with it, if he so desires, and to aid in its maintenance and preservation. The Catholic Church, then, viewed as a natural religious society and prescinding from its divine establishment is a legitimate society and is entitled at least to the rights which by nature belong to such a society.

As a religious society it differs from other societies or corporations that are called civil societies. It is true that these other societies also may exist in virtue of the natural law. Yet they are always established for a purpose that is subordinate to the general temporal welfare; the means used are naturally under the control and surveillance of the public authority; and thus the legislator, the public authority, is the judge of their usefulness, and of the danger they may offer to the general welfare. Hence the public authority is the judge also of the licitness of such societies. It can destroy them in certain circumstances, if it so wishes, in order to safeguard more important interests in the political order.[13]

The relations of the public authority with the religious society are quite different. The object towards which the civil society moves is the temporal welfare of its citizens. The end of the religious society, however, is the spiritual welfare of its members. Civil governments were not formed for religion, or for the administration of sacred things. The affairs of religion are beyond the sphere of the civil authority.[14] The Church, then, always considered as a natural society, has an object or end that is not directly subordinate to the end of the civil society. It is true that the attainment of this end is very conducive to the general temporal well-being of the citizens of the State; nevertheless, the purpose of the religious society, the spiritual welfare of men, cannot be made subordinate to that of the civil society, the merely temporal welfare of men. The religious society, therefore, possesses a certain degree of independence and freedom from the civil power.

It follows from all this that the Catholic Church, the same as any religious society, has within itself sufficient reason for its existence. The individuals who compose the Church have the right to associate in order to obtain by the use of common means an end that is legitimate and not detrimental or harmful. Their society draws its rights from the will of its members, and is limited by only one law—the duty and obligation of not impeding other societies in the exercise of their rights.[15]

[13] Moulart, *L'Eglise et L'Etat,* liv. III, ch. VIII, art. II, p. 555.

[14] Grotius, *De Imperio* (Parisiis, 1647), cap. 2, § 3; Soglia, *Institutiones Iuris Publici Ecclesiastici,* pars II, § 9.

[15] *Cf.* Fourneret on the necessity of the civil law for the formation of the religious society: "On ne voit pas ce que la loi civile peut ajouter de réal ni surtout d'essentiel à un être complet par lui-même, parfait par le concours des volontés de ceux qui le constituent et le reconstituent à chaque instant par leur accord permanent."—Dictionnaire de théologie catholique, v. "Biens Ecclesiastiques," p. 843.

C. The Right of the Church as a Religious Society to Acquire Property

From the foregoing it follows that, even if the Church be falsely considered as a human organization, it has the right to acquire property. Every man has the natural right to form a society with other men, contributing along with them his resources both physical and moral to the society in order that he may attain with their help the end which he alone would be incapable of attaining. Hence individuals have the right to found a *religious* society, so that by their united efforts they may attain their spiritual welfare, and give to God the glory due Him. But the right to form the association presupposes in the society so formed the right to acquire and possess all those things that are necesary for its existence and activity.[16]

No society can exist without property. Every legitimate society, therefore, has the right to acquire and possess those things that are necessary for it to function and exist. The Church is not different in this respect. In order to function as an external and visible society it has need of temporal goods, and in view of what has already been said, it has the right to acquire them. Even considered as a merely human or natural society (as it is, in fact, considered by many civil powers today), the Church must attain its own ends—those ends for which it was instituted; it must maintain its social life, and continue its social activity; it must maintain its security and guard its independence. All this presupposes in any society the ownership and use of temporal goods and a steady income. Hence the Church also, even if falsely considered as a merely human society, has the right to acquire these things.[17]

The Church as a religious society must have altars, and church edifices in which to carry out the proper celebration of divine worship. It must have buildings and material resources with which to assure the proper education and perpetuation of its ministers and officials. It must be able to support the charitable and pious institutions which are made necessary by its distinctive purpose as a religious society. Its needs must not be construed as

[16] De Meester, *Compendium,* III, n. 1439.

[17] Barile, *De Patrimoniali Ecclesiae Regimine* (Romae: Athenaeum, 1925), p. 4.

being restricted to those things which have a direct and immediate connection with divine worship. For as a human society, as well as a religious society, the Church has every right to those material goods which will assure its preservation and functioning.[18]

Even though the Church *de facto* and *de iure* is a supernatural society, and even though by its origin it is a divine society, it is, however, composed of men. Its members are human beings, not spirits. Because of this it has need of means proportioned to the nature of its members and hence requires temporal goods.[19] As a society of men the Church is subject to all the needs that are experienced by every society, and that cannot be met without the right to acquire and use temporal goods.[20] It is clear, then, that the Church must have the right to acquire temporal goods. It needs them in order to live.

It may be objected here that the Church, although a society of men, has been formed for a spiritual purpose. Its object is the spiritual welfare of men. For this reason it may be thought to be incapable of having the right to acquire temporal goods. It is admitted that temporal goods of themselves are inadequate to attain the supernatural end of the Church. Yet they are necessary among men in order that men may act *visibly* and *externally* in the use of other, spiritual, means.[21] Moreover, whatever may be the purpose of the Church, it always retains its juridical personality. As long as the Church is a religious society it will never lose the personality that is a natural consequence of its social being.

Here again it must be remembered that the Church is being regarded merely as a human society, as a society that draws its *raison d'etre,* its rights and its freedom of action from the perma-

[18] Cavagnis, *Diritto Publico,* n. 376; *Institutiones Iuris Publici,* III, 382, 385; Pistocchi, *De Bonis Ecclesiae Temporalibus,* p. 9; Ottaviani, *Institutiones Iuris Publici Ecclesiastici,* I, n. 198; Devoti, *Institutiones Canonicae,* II, tit. 13, § 1; Coronata, *Institutiones Iuris Canonici,* n. 1035.

[19] Cavagnis, *Diritto Publico,* n. 376; Pistocchi, *De Bonis Ecclesiae Temporalibus,* 9.

[20] Coronata, *Institutiones Iuris Canonici,* n. 1035.

[21] "Homines tendunt ad finem prout communi conspiratione attingi potest, hinc est quod societas etsi sit spiritualis et supernaturalis, ob finem, tamen ob media erit non modo spiritualis et supernaturalis, sed etiam externa et visibilis; igitur eius media adaequate inspecta oportet sint mixtae naturae."—Cavagnis, *Institutiones Iuris Publici,* I, n. 46.

nent and independent union of the wills of its members.[22] Such a society, it is maintained, has a natural right to acquire property.

The principal difficulty in this concept of the Church lies, of course, in the fact that it does not correspond to reality. It does not account for the independence of the Church's right, for if the Church be a voluntary association, founded upon a contract or covenant of fellowship, there is no reason why it should be exempted from civil jurisdiction. The American courts, however, are loath to exercise jurisdiction over ecclesiastical matters except in cases where property rights are concerned. Instead they lean toward a policy of "recognition of Church authority evidently conceded to spring from a supernatural source." [23] This view of the courts is a faint reflection of reality as far as the Catholic Church is concerned, for the Church is a divine institution and independent of the civil authority by reason of its divine establishment as a perfect society.

However, it must be remembered that the argument from natural law, as advanced by Catholic authors, seeks only to show that there exists no reason for the denial of the right of the Catholic Church to acquire property when that right is acknowledged and recognized in other associations of citizens.

In concluding this section one may well summarize the argument for the Church's right to property that is given by Carriere in his work *De Iustitia et Iure.*[24] This noted author argues that an ownership of property that involves no contradiction and is moreover necessary to the Church ought to be acknowledged as belonging to the Church. And he shows that the ownership of property by the Church fulfils these two conditions. It is true that the Church as a religious society is a society of many persons, and any property owned by the society would belong to the society

[22] *Cf.* De Meester, *Compendium,* n. 1439.

[23] "Church membership stands upon an altogether higher plane, and church membership is not to be compared to that resulting from connection with mere business associations for profit, pleasure or culture. The Church undertakes to deal with spiritual interests. Admission to its fold is prescribed alone by the Church professing to act upon the Word of God."—Nance v. Busby, 91 Tenn. 303; *cf.* Brown, Brendan F., *The Canonical Juristic Personality* (The Catholic University of America, Canon Law Studies, n. 39, Washington, D. C.: The Catholic University of America, 1927), pp. 123–126.

[24] I, n. 106.

and not to the individual members. There is no inconsistency involved in this, for even the civil law acknowledges ownership by corporations and other moral persons. Besides, man is impelled by his very nature to enter societies of various kinds. Just as the capacity of man to own property is deduced from his faculties and needs, so also the capacity of the society to own property must be recognized as arising from the same natural faculties and needs. It is also true that the Church needs property. It therefore has a right to it. For the Church has the right to those things that are necessary for her existence. Without some property it could not exist or function.

In fine, the Church viewed even as a human society has a legitimate right to exist. Consequently it has the right to acquire the means to attain the end for which it was established; hence it has also the right to acquire and to possess property.

CHAPTER IV

THE INDEPENDENT RIGHT TO PROPERTY

THE Church's right to property is not only a native right; it is also an independent right. This is to say that the Church's right to property does not arise from any concession or recognition of the State, and that in the exercise of this right the Church cannot be compelled by any human law. Even though it is not recognized by the civil law, the Church possesses it and can rightly use it. In conformity with this twofold independence this chapter is divided into two sections, of which the first discusses the origin of the independent right to property, and the second the corollary of the independent exercise of the right.

A. THE ORIGIN OF THE CHURCH'S INDEPENDENT RIGHT

The erroneous opinions that have been held regarding this point may be divided into two classes: 1) the view that acknowledges the right of the Church to acquire, retain, and administer property, but only because of a concession of the civil law; 2) the view that denies that the Church has any right to property because all temporal goods are the property of the State.

The basic principle of the latter view, *viz.*, that the ownership of all temporal goods belongs to the State, has been abandoned as unscientific.[1] It is, however, very old and has been invoked very frequently in the Church's history. St. Ambrose opposed and refuted it when he refused to obey the Emperor's order to hand over Catholic churches to the Arians.[2] Arnold of Brescia (circa 1148) invoked it in his attempt to overthrow the temporal power of the Popes in order to restore the Roman Republic to the Capitoline.[3]

A variation of the doctrine reappeared in France during the eighteenth century. Garat (+1823) held that the State was the

[1] Wernz, *Ius Decretalium,* III, n. 135; Huebler, *Der Eigenthuemer des Kirchengutes* (Leipzig, 1868), p. 71.

[2] Ep. xx, nn. 2, 18, 19—*MPL,* xvi, 994, 996, 999.

[3] *Cf.* Mansi xxi, 539; Audisio, *Droit Public de l'Eglise* (3 vols., Louvain, 1864–1865), I, tit. 33, n. 9.

actual owner of all church property. The reason he gave was the fact that the representatives of the State had for centuries exercised acts of ownership over church property. The King had nominated ecclesiastics to bishoprics and abbeys, had given his permission for alienations and acquisitions of church property, and during vacancies in benefices had taken the revenues of the benefices. Garat's facts were true, but he failed to realize that the authority exercised by the civil rulers were privileges that had been granted them by the Church.[4]

Mirabeau (+1791) also held that the State owned all church property. The property in the possession of the Church had originally been the property of the king and of the people who later had transferred it to the Church in fulfillment of their natural obligation to provide the necessary means for divine worship. The right of ownership, according to Mirabeau, came from the State. The State gave to the individual the *exclusive* right to a particular portion of property to which according to natural law everyone had an equal right.[5]

The first class of errors mentioned above, *viz.*, that which acknowledges the property rights of the Church but claims that they depend upon the supreme political power, comprises the opinions of John of Jandun (+1328), of Marsilius of Padua (+1342), and of many politicians and jurists of the eighteenth and nineteenth centuries.

John of Jandun and Marsilius of Padua held that all the temporal goods of the Church belonged *by right* to the civil ruler who could, at his pleasure, take possession of them as his own. The Church possessed them only in virtue of the authorization of the supreme political power from whom proceeded all ecclesiastical powers and rights.[6]

In the eighteenth century the attack on church property was leveled against the ecclesiastical institutions or corporations. As the theories regarding the origin of corporate personality varied,

[4] Hirschel, *Das Eigenthum am katholischen Kirchengute—AKKR*, xxxiv, (1875), pp. 38–39.

[5] *Rapports, Opinions, et Discours prononcés a la Tribune Nationale a Paris,* 1818, I, 87, 127, 135—apud Hirschel, *op. cit.*, p. 39.

[6] John XXII, Const., *"Licet iuxta doctrinam,"* 23 oct. 1327—*Denz.* 495, 500; *cf.* also Pastor, *History of the Popes,* vol. I, 3 ed., (St. Louis, 1906), p. 79.

so did the attack on church corporations. The aim of the theorists and politicians who led the attack was to give a veneer of legality to the spoliation of church property. The opinion voiced by Thouret (+1794) is characteristic of the legal view of his time. Thouret reasoned that corporations within the State obtained their right to own property only from the State. The State could withdraw this right to itself if it so desired, and in this manner could repossess the corporation's property. This view was developed and popularized by the Encyclopedists. It greatly influenced Louis XVI's ministers, Turgot (+1787) and Malesherbes (+1794), who sought to appropriate all church property by means of it. In fact, the confiscation of church property that occurred in Europe after the French revolution was founded upon this theory.[7]

In the nineteenth century this theory was frequently repeated by authors according to whom the juridical personality of the Church, in virtue of which it had the right to property, was granted by the State. The Church was regarded like any other corporation as a creature of the civil law and subject to its provisions. It could exist and function as long as the law allowed. Should the law ever deprive it of its civil personality it would cease to be and would lose all its rights under the law, including the right to property.[8] If this should happen, church property would become *res nullius,* and hence the State would legally succeed to its ownership.[9]

All these theories are to be rejected. The theory that all property belongs by right to the civil authority is no longer held, but the theory that the State is the source of the juridical personality and capacity of the Church is still widely held outside the Church. The provisions of Roman law are quoted in support of

[7] Hirschel, *Das Eigenthum am katholischen Kirchengute—AKKR,* xxxiv (1875), 39.

[8] *Cf.* Moulart, *L'Eglise et L'Etat,* liv. III, ch. VIII, art. II; Liberatore, *L'Eglise et L'Etat,* liv. II, ch. II. Hergenroether-Hollweck (*Lehrbuch des katholischen Kirchenrechts,* n. 1020) name the following as among those who regard church property rights as a mere concession of the State: Richter-Dove, Hinschius, Friedberg, Bolgeni, Walter, Evelt, Poschinger, Meurer, Gross. Many of these authors, however, admit that the Church is entitled in equity to such a concession of the State.

[9] Friedberg, *Lehrbuch des katholischen und evangelischen Kirchenrechts,* § 175.

this latter theory, and it is argued that the Church itself asked for and obtained from the Roman State the juridical capacity to acquire and possess property.[10] It is true that until the edict of Constantine (312 or 313) the Church was an illegal society under the Roman law [11] and consequently its rights as a society were not previously recognized by the law. Nevertheless, the Church in virtue of its native right acquired, possessed, and administered property. In several instances its ownership was legally protected and to a certain extent recognized by the civil authorities.[12] When peace was restored to the Church Constantine recognized the juridical personality of the Church and the consequent right to acquire temporal goods. His edicts did not grant privileges, as Friedberg claims.[13] They recognized a right already belonging to the Church. The law merely conferred the legal protection of the State upon the rights of the Church.[14]

It has been said that under the Roman law juridical personality was a concession of the State.[15] Today it is admitted that the concession of juridical personality as a condition of the existence of any society was not known before the late empire.[16] According to the Digests the juridical personality was a natural consequence of the fact of the union of the members. The law really prohibited the formation of societies; but once the society was formed, the law recognized its natural right to acquire and possess property.[17] No express recognition of the society by the State was necessary.

It is curious that Roman law should have been put forth as the basis of a theory that sought to justify the spoliation of church property. When the Roman law dissolved an illicit society the property of the society did not become *res nullius,* as the modern

[10] Friedberg, *Lehrbuch,* § 167.

[11] *Cf.* D(47.22) 1.

[12] *Cf.* Eusebius, *Historia Ecclesiastica* VII, 13; VII, 30; VIII, 17—*MPG,* xx, 674, 719, 794.

[13] *Lehrbuch,* § 167.

[14] Lactantius, *De Mortibus Persecutorum,* cap. 48—*MPL,* VII, 270; C(1.2) 1.

[15] Friedberg, *Lehrbuch,* §§ 167, 175.

[16] Moulart, *L'Eglise et L'Etat,* liv. iii, ch. viii, art. i.

[17] D(47.22) 3, 4. *Cf.* Bonfante, *Istituzioni di Diritto Romano,* p. 66, note (1).

jurists would wish, but reverted to the members.[18] If this provision of Roman law had been applied in the dissolution of monasteries and convents, then church property would not have become the property of the State, but would have been distributed among the religious.

Among the more recent authors the principle argument against the independent right of the Church remains unchanged: the Church has no legal personality other than that granted by the civil state.[19] Although some authors concede that the universal Church possesses juridical personality in public law, they maintain that such personality cannot give rise to property rights, for within the boundaries of the State the civil law reigns supreme and all questions of property are to be settled according to the particular laws of the separate states.[20]

To acknowledge, as these jurists do, that the Church has juridical personality in public law, and at the same time to assert that *in concreto* the Church cannot own property except by concession of the civil law is at least contradictory. Such a view assumes that corporations (*i. e.,* moral persons) cannot exist except in virtue of civil law. But such an assumption is false. What divine or natural law has established human law cannot set aside. There can be and there are moral persons that actually exist and have a real legitimate right to exist, to acquire, and to possess according to divine and natural law. The Church has moral personality in virtue of divine law. Hence the Church does not depend on the civil law for its juridical personality and its property rights.[21]

From the establishment of the Church as a perfect society, it is clear that Christ intended that His Church possess the independent

[18] D(47.22) 3; Fourneret in *Dictionnaire de Théologie Catholique,* s.v. "Biens Ecclésiastiques."

[19] Meurer, *Begriff und Eigenthuemer der heiligen Sachen;* Huebler, *Der Eigenthuemer des Kirchengutes;* Friedberg, *Lehrbuch des katholischen und evangelischen Kirchenrechts;* Poschinger, *Das Eigenthum am Kirchenvermoegen.*

[20] *E. g.,* Hinschius as quoted by Meurer, *Begriff und Eigenthuemer,* I, p. 10, note 6; Von Sybel, *Das Altkatholische Bistum,* p. 4; Huebler, *Der Eigenthuemer des Kirchengutes,* p. 151.

[21] Hirschel, *Das Eigenthum am katholischen Kirchengute—AKKR,* xxxiv (1875), 84; idem, *Sind bischoefliche Ordinariate erbfaehig?—AKKR,* xxvii (1871), 23–42.

right to acquire the means necessary for the work He gave it to do. The Church, according to Christ's will, is a perfect society independent of every other society. To say that its right to acquire and administer property comes from the civil law is to make it dependent upon the civil power, and to place it in servitude.[22]

In his discussion of this point Liberatore[23] writes: "Is the Church composed of men? Have men the right to possess? Can the possessor dispose of his possessions as he wishes? Certainly, provided the rights of others are not violated. Now, the Church is a society composed of men who are independent owners of temporal goods; it must, then, be acknowledged that the Church has the independent right of ownership. No one would say that the members can possess, but not the society; for, from the moment that the society exists, it enjoys all the natural rights that are given it by the principle that has formed it and the will of its members—always provided that neighboring societies are never harmed. Now, both the principle that gives form to the Church and the will of its members carry with them the right to property. Hence the Church regarded as a natural society, has the right to possess independently of positive law."

No one would deny that property owners can unite in order to obtain an obligatory moral or spiritual good, and that in the society which they form they can hold all or part of their property in common. Now, supposing this right to form a society, one must admit an authority in the established society, and acknowledge the right of the authority to unite the external efforts of the members to obtain the end for which the society was established. Hence the authority can designate the proper means to be used, and direct the members in their use. Among such means are temporal goods, money, property. These goods, then, fall under the social authority of the society—in this case the Church—and nothing

[22] Cavagnis, *Diritto Publico,* n. 309; Hergenroether-Hollweck, *Lehrbuch des katholisches Kirchenrechts,* n. 1022; Pistochi, *De Bonis Ecclesiae Temporalibus,* p. 14; Hirschel, *Das Eigenthum am katholischen Kirchengute —AKKR,* XXXIV (1875), 84. On the Church's divine right to property confer the following authors quoted by Meurer, *Begriff und Eigenthuemer,* I, 7; Helle, *Das kirchliche Vermoegen,* p. 5; Hergenroether, *Katholische Kirche und christlicher Staat,* p. 115; Affre, *Traité de la Propriété des Biens Ecclésiastiques,* p. 8.

[23] *L'Eglise et L'Etat,* liv. III, ch. III.

but this authority can regulate the manner in which they are to be used for the good of the society. It follows from this that the members, if they so desire, can dispose of their property for the benefit of the society; and the society to whom these goods are given can possess them lawfully.

Now, if the Church possesses property in view of the end it ought to attain it also has the right to administer it. Not to acknowledge this right would be to rank the Church with the insane, or to consider the society, to whom millions entrust the care of their souls, incapable of administering temporal goods.[24]

The origin of the Church's independent right to property is further evidenced from the fact that Christ willed His Church to be subject in no wise to the State. If in accordance with Christ's will the Church is not to be subject to the civil authority, its right to acquire and administer property is an independent right. It is inconceivable that Christ should wish His Church to be independent of the State, and at the same time desire that it derive its juridical personality and rights from the State.

Christ willed that His Church should not depend directly upon the State. This is to be concluded from the very nature of the end of the Church, man's salvation, which is something beyond the scope and ability of the civil authority. Moreover, Christ's own words exclude such direct dependence. He said to Peter: "Thou art Peter; and upon this rock I will build my church, and the gates of hell shall not prevail against it. And I will give to thee the keys of the kingdom of heaven. And whatsoever thou shalt bind upon earth, it shall be bound also in heaven; and whatsoever thou shalt loose on earth, it shall be loosed also in heaven." [25] Christ asserted universally and absolutely (not conditionally) that whatever Peter bound on earth would be bound in heaven, and whatever Peter loosed on earth would be loosed in heaven. Peter's authority evidently was supreme, independent; not subject to further revision by any human power. For if it were subject to the civil power—that is, lawfully, juridically, subject—the civil power would loose what Peter had bound, and what God in heaven had ratified. In this hypothesis the civil power could lawfully and authoritatively decide on the acts of the Church and could lawfully

[24] Taparelli, *Saggio Teoretico di Dritto Naturale*, nn. 1471–1472.

[25] Matthew, xvi, 18–19.

and authoritatively nullify them; and God would either ratify the State's decision and not Peter's, or else he would ratify Peter's decision and the State could lawfully nullify God's ratification! It is evident, then, that the government of the Church was to be absolutely independent of the civil power.

Furthermore, Christ's Church was to be universal; and it was to be united, one. Christ intended that it should be governed by Peter to whom He committed the care of His entire flock. If, however, the Church depended upon the civil power, then the supreme power in the Church would be held by the various governments throughout the world. It would have no unity.[26]

Finally, when entrusting the government of His Church to human beings, Christ made no mention of the civil power. His words were directed solely to Peter. Peter was given complete power and authority. If the juridical personality and authority of the Church were dependent upon the civil power, the Church could not have existed before the fourth century. There were no Christian rulers at the time of the establishment of the Church, nor for the first three centuries of its existence. On the contrary, the rulers of the first three hundred years were for the most part hostile to Christianity. When Christian emperors came into power the bishops did not relinquish their power to the civil authorities, nor was the authority of the religious rulers *ipso facto* abrogated in favor of the civil rulers. Rather, the emperors themselves acknowledged the juridical competence of the Church in all matters pertaining to ecclesiastical government; and when they forgot, they were very forcefully reminded by the bishops.[27]

"The government of the Church is supernatural and belongs to no one but those to whom God has committed it. We read in Scripture that it was committed to The Apostles and to their successors the bishops. To Peter it was said: Feed my sheep (John xxi, 17) and of bishops it is said: God the Holy Ghost hath placed you bishops to rule the Church of God (Acts, xx, 28). We never read the like about kings." [28]

[26] *Cf.* De Meester, *Compendium,* I, n. 150.

[27] *E. g.,* St. Ambrose, *Ep. xx,* nn. 2, 8, 19—*MPL,* xvi, 994, 996, 999; St. John Damascene, *Oratio ii,* n. 12—*MPG,* xciv, 1295–1298; Synod of Rome (502)—c. 1, D. xcvi.

[28] Bellarmine, *De Romano Pontifice,* I, cap. 7—*Opera Omnia* (8 vols., Neapoli, 1872), I, 320.

From the foregoing it is clear that Christ's intention was that His Church should not depend directly upon the civil society. It should be independent; it should stand alone, endowed as it was with sufficient power and authority to fulfill the purpose for which it had been established.

Since the Church as a society was established independently of the civil power, its rights as a moral person are not derived from the civil law but from the authority that established it, *viz.,* the power and will of Jesus Christ. In particular, the right to acquire property, to have and to hold temporal goods, is not subject to the civil authority but only to divine law and to the regulations of the Church authority.[29]

Christ willed that His Church should not depend even indirectly upon the State. This indirect dependence would manifest itself if the purpose and end of the ecclesiastical society—free and independent in its own order—were found to be subject to and subordinate to the purpose and end of the civil society. But it is evident that Christ gave His Church a purpose, an end vastly superior to that of the civil society. Hence it cannot be said that His Church is dependent even indirectly upon the civil society. From this it must be clear that Christ's evident will was that His Church be absolutely independent of the civil society. As such it is impossible that the Church depend upon the civil society for the very means necessary for its end, *viz.,* the right to acquire and administer temporal goods.

The State has a duty to acknowledge the independent position of the Church, and to recognize its rights and to afford them the protection of its laws. As long as the civil power does not recognize the personality of the Church and its institutions and their native capacity to acquire and administer temporal goods, church property remains without external guarantee and security. The divine and natural rights of the Church are rendered ineffectual and inadequate. According to Moulart[30] the State has a threefold obligation to recognize the juridical capacity of the Church. It has a duty toward the Church, since the powers of both come from God Who has thus intimated the obligation of mutual recognition.

[29] Liberatore, *L'Eglise et L'Etat,* liv. III, ch. III; Wernz, *Ius Decretalium,* III, n. 136; Ottaviani, *Institutiones Iuris Publici Ecclesiastici,* I, n. 199.

[30] *L'Eglise et L'Etat,* liv. III, ch. VIII, art. II.

It has a duty toward itself, inasmuch as it is to the best interests of the civil society that the rights of the Church be guaranteed by the law. It has a duty toward its citizens who, recognizing and accepting the truth of the Christian Religion, wish to preserve it, and can, therefore, demand that the civil power assure its existence and prosperity.

The least that can be done by the State is to assure the Church the right to acquire property in all the ways by which its own subjects can acquire. The Church on its part subjects itself and its institutions to the formalities of the civil law in property transactions [81] in order to obtain legal protection and to maintain peace and avoid unnecessary collision with the civil authority.

Yet, although in acquiring and retaining possession of temporal goods the Church *de facto* follows the civil law regarding conditions and formalities, or even requires the observance of the civil law in the ecclesiastical forum, it is not strictly obliged to do so, and always reserves the basic right to acquire and possess in virtue of its divinely given native and independent right.[82]

B. The Independent Exercise of the Church's Right

From the origin of the independent property rights of the Church it follows that the Church is independent of the State in the exercise of its right. This independence is referred to in a general way by Pope Leo XIII: "Sicut finis quo tendit Ecclesia longe nobilissimus est, ita eius potestas est omnium praestantissima, neque imperio civili potest haberi inferior, aut eidem esse ullo modo obnoxia . . . Ecclesiam in suorum officiorum munere potestati civili velle esse subiectam, magna quidem iniuria, magna temeritas est. Hoc facto perturbatur ordo, quia quae naturalia sunt praeponuntur iis quae sunt supra naturam." [83]

Since the Church is a sovereign society, recognized as such by the many civil governments that have signed concordats, and has been endowed by its Founder with all the means necessary to attain its end, it is civilly autonomous. It determines of itself the

[81] Canons 1508; 1513, § 2; 1523, n. 2; 1529.

[82] *Cf.* c. 11, X, *de testamentis et ultimis voluntatibus,* III, 26; can. 1513, § 2.

[83] Ep. encycl. *"Immortale Dei,"* 1, nov. 1885, §§ 5, 15—*Fontes,* n. 592.

modes of acquisition, the legal forms to be observed and the regulations to be followed in transfers of property between its own institutions. It is not inherently bound by civil law in these matters. The Decretals amply testify to the autonomy of the Church in regard to the exercise of its property rights,[34] and recent concordats recognize the right of the Church to acquire property by any just title whatsoever (*quovis iusto titulo*).[35]

If at times the Church has agreed to observe the formalities required by the civil law, it has done so not out of necessity, but freely and for reasonable causes. In all such cases it insists on its native right to acquire and administer, even though for reasons of prudence it sees fit to relinquish the exercise of that right.[36] When the Church has not made special concessions, however, it insists upon its native and independent right. Thus, although canon law provides that bequests to the Church be made according to the formalities required by the civil law, canon law asserts that if the formalities have been omitted the heirs are to be admonished of their duty to fulfill the will of the testator.[37] The Church can acquire temporal goods in any just manner that by natural or positive law is allowed to others; [38] it is free to accept the voluntary offerings of the faithful,[39] and to impose taxes if necessary.[40] Religious societies, provinces, and houses are also capable of acquiring property in any just and licit way. The only limitation is that which is placed on them by their rules and constitutions.[41] Similar law governs pious associations.[42]

[34] X, III, 14–24, 26, 27.

[35] *E. g.*, art. 17 of concordat with Costa Rica (1852) ; art. 18, Guatemala (1852) ; art. 29, Austria (1855) ; art. 17, San Salvador (1862) ; art. 22, Venezuela (1862)—Mercati, *Raccolta di Concordati* (Roma: Tipografia Poliglotta Vaticana, 1919), pp. 806, 818, 827, 967, 977.

[36] *Cf.* concordats cited above; also art. 19, Ecuador (1881) ; art. 5 Colombia (1887)—*Raccolta*, pp. 1011, 1052; art. 16, Poland (1925)—*AAS*, XVII (1925), p. 279; art. 17, Lithuania (1927)—*AAS*, XIX (1927), p. 431.

[37] C. 1513, § 2.

[38] C. 1499, § 1.

[39] Cc. 691, §§ 1, 2; 1182, §§ 2, 3.

[40] C. 1496; *cf.* also Pius X, ep. "*Acre nefariumque,*" 14 maii 1905—*Fontes*, n. 668.

[41] C. 531.

[42] C. 691, §§ 1, 2.

C. The Spoliation of Church Property

If the Church has the right to acquire and possess property, it follows that the usurpation or spoliation of church property is a violation of church rights. This crime, however, does not always violate the native right of the Church. It is possible for the usurper to appropriate to himself a portion of the Church's property and still recognize the native right of the Church. If, however, the spoliation is defended, for example, by the theory that church rights to property are merely a concession of the civil law which has now withdrawn them, the native right of the Church would be violated. The Church claims the inherent right to property, independent of the civil law, a right that belongs to it by virtue of its divine establishment as a perfect society.[43] Hence the State cannot arbitrarily apply church property to its own ends without grievously offending the rights of the Church; nor can it claim the right of escheat in the case wherein a certain piece of church property can no longer be applied to its immediate end. The Church alone is empowered to dispose of the property dedicated to religious purposes.[44]

D. Mortmain Statutes

Mortmain statutes is the name given to those laws, introduced in medieval times, that prohibit the transfer of temporal goods, especially real estate, to the ownership of the Church without consent of the civil ruler. In the first statutes of mortmain are to be seen the earliest traces in English law of opposition to the rights of the Church regarding the acquisition of property. Primarily intended to protect the rights of feudal lords, and especially the crown, the mortmain laws actually violated the rights of the Church, by restricting her power to acquire. Under the feudal system the vassal land-owner was bound to render certain services, *e. g.*, military aid, to his lord. Naturally these feudal services could be rendered only if the vassal was a physical person. If a juridical person like a monastery or a church owned the lands, the services that hitherto had been due from such fiefs

[43] Liberatore, *L'Eglise et L'Etat,* liv. III, ch. III.
[44] Wernz-Vidal, *Ius Canonicum,* IV, n. 744.

were withdrawn and, as the subject was incapable of committing crime and would never die, the fee would never escheat to the lord. Consequently he lost considerable revenue. The feudal system required vassals to pay taxes to their lords at certain times, *e. g.*, upon the marriage of the lord's daughter, or the knighting of his son. Since a monastery would never exact taxes of this sort, land-owners were not loath to transfer their property to a monastery with a view that they might receive it back as a fief. Thus they became vassals of the religious corporation and enjoyed the use of their property much as they had before the transfer, while the monastery became the feudal lord and owner. Since, therefore, lands held by church corporations never escheated to the feudal lord, and never provided the feudal revenues that a lay vassal would have been required to pay, church corporations were called *"manus mortuae,"* and every acquisition of property by them was considered a detriment to the secular prince.

Lest the possession of property by such *manus mortuae* increase, the civil rulers passed laws that either forbade the transfer of property to the Church or required their previous permission, sometimes for every acquisition of property by the Church, sometimes for the acquisition of property above a certain value.[45]

Before the advent of mortmain statutes the feudal lords sought to solve the problem of the increasing ownership of corporate bodies by seizing the revenues of vacant benefices.[46] Although the benefices were held under Church tenure from the feudal lords themselves, they did not escheat to the lord upon becoming vacant. The lord probably regarded the seized revenues as belonging to him in lieu of the income he would have received had he been able to bestow the benefice as a fief on some vassal. Local councils legislated against this practice and the king himself was even prevailed upon to forbid it by law.[47] But the mortmain statutes

[45] *Cf.* Mann, *Lives of the Popes,* XVIII (London, 1932), 236; Hannan, *The Canon Law of Wills,* Catholic University of America, Canon Law Studies, n. 86 (Washington, D. C.: The Catholic University of America, 1934), n. 539.

[46] Council of Meaux (845)—Harduin, IV, 1486; Thomassinus, *Vetus et Nova Ecclesiae Disciplina* (3 vols., Paris, 1688), Pars III, lib. II, cap. 54. Hereafter reference to this work is implied with the mention of Thomassinus.

[47] Council of Mainz (813), c. 50—Harduin, IV, 1016; Council of Reims (813), c. 24—Harduin, IV, 1020; Council of Meaux (845), cc. 17, 22—Harduin, IV, 1486; Thomassinus, Pars III, lib. II, cap. 54, 55.

represent the first attempt to solve the problem by interfering with the Church's native right to acquire. Although their primary purpose was to preserve the feudal rights of the king and the other lords, in reality they sought to attain this purpose by a violation of the inherent right of the Church to acquire and possess property.

One of the earliest English statutes forbade the devising of land to religious corporations. This was a device by which the donor gave the land to the corporation with the agreement that he was to use it during his lifetime just as if he were the real owner. Upon his death the corporation attained full feudal ownership. Henry III (1216–1272) forbade this in his Magna Carta.[48]

The statute of Edward I (1272–1307), *de viris religiosis,* prohibited the practice of transferring land to a religious corporation and immediately receiving it back as a fief, and ordained that "no religious or any other person shall buy or sell lands or tenements or receive them (under pain of forfeiture) so as to cause the land to come into mortmain (per quod ad manum mortuam terrae et tenementa huius modi deveniant quoquo modo)." [49]

The Statute of Westminster forbade religious houses or communities to acquire property by common recovery. Richard II (1377–1399) prohibited conveyances of land in trust for religious corporations except by permission of the crown.[50]

These statutes are mentioned merely to illustrate how mortmain statutes restricted the right of the Church to acquire property. The same statutes acknowledged the legality of ecclesiastical ownership,[51] but prohibited future acquisition of real property by ecclesiastical corporations.

The statute of Henry VIII (1509–1547) more directly violated

[48] "Non licet alicui de cetero dare terram suam alicui domui religiosae, ita quod illam resumat tenendam de eadem domo; nec liceat alicui domui religiosae terram alicuius sic accipere, quod tradat illam ei a quo ipsam recepit tenendam; si quis autem de caetero terram suam domui religiosae sic dederit, et super hoc convincatur, donum suum penitus cassetur, ut terra illa domino suo illius feodi incurratur."—Evans, *A Collection of Statutes* (London, 1817), I, 343; 9 Henry III, 36.

[49] Hannan, *Canon Law of Wills,* nn. 541, 542; Mann, *Lives of the Popes,* XVIII, chap. VII, p. 236.

[50] Hannan, *Canon Law of Wills,* nn. 544, 547.

[51] *E. g.,* 15 Richard II, c. 5—Hannan, *op. cit.,* n. 547.

the right of the Church. It forbade future grants of land to be held for superstitious uses even if held in trust by the heirs of the donor (unless the trust would not endure for twenty years).[52] The Chantries Act of 1547 invalidated all grants or gifts of property to the Church or religious institutions.[53]

The French laws required the Church to pay a tax for the mere acquisition of property. The law of 1275 specified this tax as the value of one year's revenue if the lands had been given to the Church; and the value of two years' revenue if the lands had been bought. The law of 1291 distinguished likewise between property that had been acquired gratis and property that had not been so acquired. The value of four years' revenue was to be given the king for permission to obtain property by a free gift; otherwise the tax was the value of three years' revenue; but if the church had paid for the acquired property in silver the tax was the value of four to six years' revenue.[54] All these mortmain laws did not actually deny the right of the Church to acquire property. They controlled the right. Either they made it impossible for church corporations to acquire lands, or if they allowed the acquisition of possessions they did so only upon the condition that permission had been granted by the civil power. For such permission a definite and determined tax was to be paid to the royal treasury.

In this way the civil authorities sought to limit the right of the Church to acquire temporal goods. By so doing the civil power assumed authority in a matter in which the Church had often declared laymen had no right to legislate or dispose.[55] Such laws have always been regarded by the Church as an unjust limitation and a violation of her native rights. The Popes have maintained that the civil government, unless it has the consent of the ecclesiastical authorities, has no power to subject ecclesiastical institutions to mortmain statutes. Boniface VIII (1294–1303) [56] stated the

[52] Evans, *A Collection of Statutes,* I, 349; Hannan, *op. cit.,* n. 548.

[53] Hannan, *op. cit.,* n. 548.

[54] Hericourt, *Les Loix Ecclésiastiques* (Paris, 1771), part. H, ch. III, p. 217.

[55] *Cf.* c. 1, D. XCVI; Anselmi Luccensis *Collectio Canonum* (Ed. Thaner, Innsbruck, 1906–1915), Lib. V, cc. 8–10; also *infra,* chap. V.

[56] Const., *"Clericis Laicos,"* 24 febr. 1296—c. 3, *de immunitate ecclesiarum,* III, 23, in VI°.

principle that lay rulers are not competent to legislate regarding church property; and in more modern times concordats have insisted that church institutions be exempted from the provisions of the mortmain laws.[57]

The Church as a perfect society has a right to all the means needful for the accomplishment of its work. The acquisition of temporal goods is nothing more than the acquisition of the means necessary for the work of the Church. Just as the State is not competent to define or limit the work of the Church, so it is incompetent to judge the quantity or the quality of the means needed for the accomplishment of that work. Only the Church itself is competent in this matter, for in the exercise of its divine rights the Church enjoys a unique competency and is not subject to any human society. If the State, therefore, limits the ability of the Church to acquire property, it violates the liberty and the rights of the divinely established religious society.[58]

Hence, those who, like Schenkl,[59] think that mortmain laws may be just in certain circumstances, are in error. It is possible that an ever increasing amount of church property would become injurious to the State. It is conceivable that enormous ecclesiastical estates would be an obstacle to the desired division of property and to the free activity of all citizens. Yet, the remedy for such conditions is not in mortmain statutes which violate the rights of the Church, but in a peaceful settlement between the Church and the State. The existence of church property is in no way harmful to the State. The old charge that religious corporations do not cultivate their lands well and as a result injure the economic standards of the country, will not stand in the light of historical fact. The truth is, as Cappello points out,[60] that there has been greater prosperity where property was held by ecclesiastical institutions.[61]

[57] *E. g.*, Modena (1841); Sicily (1818), art. 15—*Raccolta*, 742, 628.

[58] Moulart, *L'Eglise et L'Etat*, liv. III, ch. VIII, art. II; Pirhing, *Ius Canonicum*, tit. de Constit. II, § 2; Soglia, *Institutiones Iuris Publici Ecclesiastici*, II, § 69; Hergenroether-Hollweck, *Lehrbuch*, n. 1029; De Meester, *Compendium*, III, n. 1441; Cavagnis, *Institutiones Iuris Publici Ecclesiastici*, III, 390.

[59] *Institutiones Iuris Ecclesiastici* (2 vols., Landishuti, 1830), § 374.

[60] *Summa iuris publici ecclesiastici* (Romae, 1928), n. 435.

[61] *Cf.* Cavagnis, *Institutiones Iuris Publici*, n. 387–388; Liberatore, *L'Eglise et L'Etat*, liv. III, ch. III, p. 277.

It is not logical to argue that because the Church forbids the alienation of property which it has acquired, the State can do likewise on account of public welfare. There is no parity in the two cases. The mortmain laws forbid the laity to transfer any part of their property to the Church. Laymen may dispose of their property in any way they wish provided that they do not confer any of it upon an ecclesiastical institution. The church law prohibiting alienation does not forbid the clergy to dispose of their own personal property in any way they wish. It merely forbids clergymen to alienate church property, of which they do not have the ownership, without the proper authorization.[62] Therefore the civil statutes of mortmain are in themselves unjust and harmful to the Church, unless ecclesiastical authorities have previously given their consent, or unless special provision has been made, *e. g.*, by concordat.[63]

[62] C. 1530, § 1.

[63] Wernz, *Ius Decretalium,* III (Romae, 1908), n. 136; Wernz-Vidal, *Ius Canonicum,* IV, n. 738.—It may be of interest to quote here a general summary of the disabilities affecting beneficiaries of charitable and religious bequests in the United States. The restrictions are suggested in the following general conclusion given by Dr. J. D. Hannan (*Canon Law of Wills,* n. 641): "First, charitable and religious bequests can be so made that they can be sustained in all the States, except Mississippi, where only bequests of personalty can be made, and even these not to religious purposes; and Wisconsin, where *devises* can not be made except to charitable and religious *corporations.* Second, it is always preferable to name a religious or charitable chartered corporation as beneficiary. Third, a trustee should be appointed, though this procedure is not sufficient in Maryland; while in Virginia, the trustee must not be an unincorporated association. Fourth, the incapacities touching clergymen and churches must be considered in Maryland, Vermont, Delaware and Louisiana. Fifth, attention must be paid to the nullifying period preceding death within which a valid charitable bequest can not be made in Pennsylvania, California, Montana, Idaho, Ohio, and Georgia. Sixth, the statutes limiting aggregate charitable bequests to a certain portion of the estate should be studied in California, Georgia, Idaho, Montana, Iowa, Louisiana, and New York. And seventh, the restrictions on the amount of property that may be held by religious and charitable institutions should be scrutinized in Pennsylvania, Massachusetts, New Hampshire, Louisiana, Arkansas, Kentucky, Tennessee, Virginia, West Virginia, and the District of Columbia."

CHAPTER V

HISTORICAL CONSPECTUS OF THE RIGHT OF THE CHURCH TO ACQUIRE PROPERTY

A. The First Exercise of the Right to Acquire

The right of the Church to own and to acquire temporal goods was not asserted in Apostolic times. The records of those times, however, abound with references to the actual ownership and management of property by ecclesiastical authorities. Such records are an indirect indication, therefore, of the right of the Church to acquire property.

The first traces of Church property according to the Fathers of the Church are to be found in the possessions of Jesus Christ and His Apostles. The Founder of the Church used temporal goods to support Himself and the Apostles and to aid the poor and the needy.[1] The Acts of the Apostles show that the early Church possessed a common fund from which were supplied the needs of the early Christians and the wants of the poor. The offerings of the faithful were accepted by the Apostles as offerings made to God for the needs of the growing society. The property was considered as belonging not to the individuals, but to the society of the faithful.[2] It was managed in the name of the Church; and ministers were appointed to dispose of it.[3] As Gregory XVI (1831–1846) has said, this acquisition and administration of temporal goods is not to be considered an invasion of the rights of others; but rather an exercise of the Church's own native right.[4]

The example of the Apostles in administering the goods of their churches was later imitated by the other churches during the first centuries of Christianity. The churches in Asia Minor, Rome, and Africa possessed funds out of which the poor and the needy were cared for and the clergy were supported. Although the Christians did not continue to hold property in common, they contributed of

[1] Mark, vi, 37; Luke, ix, 13; John, iv, 8; xii, 6; xiii, 29.

[2] Acts, ii, 44; iv, 34–37; v, 4.

[3] Acts, vi, 1–6.

[4] Allocut., "*Afflictas,*" 1 mart. 1841—*Fontes,* n. 496.

their possessions to a general fund out of which the needs of the Church were supplied.[5]

There are several indications that the Church at this period possessed not only funds for the relief of the poor and other movable goods, but also immovable property. Hippolytus (+235) mentions that Pope Zephyrinus (198–217) recalled Calixtus to Rome to take charge of the cemetery that now bears his name.[6] Pope Fabian, who ruled the Church from 236 to 250, undertook a program of construction in the cemeteries for the convenience of Christian worship.[7] In the time of Pope Cornelius (circa 251) the Church of Rome is described as supporting 44 priests, 14 deacons and subdeacons, 94 other clerics, and 1500 virgins and poor. A considerable amount of property must have been necessary to sustain all these persons and at the same time to allow the Roman Church to send alms to remote regions.[8] The Roman Emperors themselves, at times, recognized the fact that the Church owned property. Gallienus (260–268) revoked the edicts of Valerian (253–260) and restored the cemeteries and other real estate to the Christians.[9] Later the Emperor Galerius (305–311) issued a similar edict that restored their churches and houses of worship.[10] The celebrated judgment of the Emperor Aurelian (270–275) in the case of Paul of Samosata (272) is a further indication of Church ownership of property. After Paul had been deposed by the Synod of Antioch (268) he refused to give up the episcopal residence and the other Church property. The orthodox element appealed to the emperor who decided that the property should be restored to those who were in communion with the Bishop of Rome.[11]

All these restorations were made to the bishops. Thus it is

[5] Justin Martyr, *Apologia,* I, 14—*MPG,* VI, 347; Tertullian, *Apologeticus,* ch. 39—*MPL,* I, 470; Eusebius, *Historia Ecclesiastica,* IV, 23—*MPG,* XX, 387.

[6] *Philosophoumenon,* IX, 12—*MPG,* XVI ter, 3384.

[7] "Hic regiones dividit diaconibus et fecit VII subdiacones . . . et multas fabricas per cymiteria fieri praecepit."—Duchesne, *Le Liber Pontificalis* (2 vols., Paris, 1886), I, 148.

[8] Eusebius, *Hist. Eccl.,* VI, 43—*MPG,* XX, 622.

[9] Eusebius, *Hist. Eccl.,* VII, 13—*MPG,* XX, 674.

[10] Eusebius, *Hist. Eccl.,* VIII, 17—*MPG,* XX, 794.

[11] Eusebius, *Hist. Eccl.,* VII, 30—*MPG,* XX, 719.

seen that the property belonged to the Church and not to private individuals.[12] The question, however, is not one of Church ownership, but rather one of the rights by which the Church acquired and possessed property. The absence of any formal recognition of the Church as a legal person in the law of the Empire further complicates the problem. Moreover, the Church was an illegal and illegitimate religious society. In the eyes of the law the Christian community as an independent religious group was absolutely incapable of acquiring and possessing property, especially land.

In the second century a rescript of Septimus Severus (193–211) allowed burial associations (*collegia funeraticia*) to be formed throughout the Empire under certain conditions. The associations were granted legal personality. They could therefore acquire property and in the event of a dispute over ownership the law afforded them a certain degree of protection. It is the opinion of De Rossi that the Christians took advantage of the facilities offered by the Emperor's rescript.[13] Cemeteries, and perhaps other possessions, became the property of the Christian burial societies. Accordingly, Church property was held by a legally recognized body. But although property so held was protected by Roman law, the right of the Church, as such, to acquire and to own property was not recognized at all. The protection of the Roman law was extended to Church property held by burial associations, not because the property belonged to the Church but because it belonged to a legal charitable society. The Christian Church as a religious society remained illegal. However, from the fact that even before any legal recognition had been extended to it the Church received the offerings of the faithful and possessed property, both movable and immovable, it is logical to infer that it was conscious—even if only in a dim way—of its right independently of the Empire and its law to acquire and to own temporal goods.

It was in virtue of this right, then, and not because of any con-

[12] Scheys, *De Iure Ecclesiae Acquirendi et Possidendi,* p. 107.

[13] *Roma sotteranea cristiana* (3 vols., Roma, 1864–1877), I, 101–103. This opinion is not shared by Duchesne, *Early History of the Christian Church* (New York, 1909), pp. 279–280, or Battifol, *Primitive Catholicism* (New York, 1911), pp. 34–36, and has been recently challenged by Roberti, "Le associazioni funerarie cristiane e la proprietà ecclesiastica nei primi tre secoli,"—*Pubblicazioni della Università Cattolica del S. Cuore;* Serie Settima—Scienze giuridiche, Milano, 1928.

cession or grant of the Roman Emperors that the Church acquired and possessed property.[14]

B. The Right to Acquire in Roman Law

Before the edict of Constantine (313) the Church had acquired property. Even though the Roman law did not recognize the society of Christians, temporal goods were acquired and held by the society, not by private individuals. This state of things was recognized by the edict of Constantine which ordered the restoration of property not to individual Christians alone, but chiefly to the society of the Christians and "to the Churches." This was a clear recognition of a juridical personality distinct from that of the individual members of the Church.[15] The edict granted no new right, but recognized an old right already possessed and exercised by the Church.[16]

Once the juridical nature of the Church had been recognized and its property restored, it became clear that the civil law recognized its right to acquire property. Specifically the Church was recognized as capable of receiving legacies,[17] a right that was not

[14] *Confutazione degli Errori e Calunnie contro La Chiesa e La Sovranità* (anonymous), (2 vols., 1794), II, ch. IX, 208–209; Hergenroether-Hollweck, *Lehrbuch,* n. 1021; Wernz-Vidal, *Ius Canonicum,* IV, n. 185; Liberatore, *Droit Public de l'Eglise,* n. 238.

[15] "Quae omnia corpori Christianorum protinus per intercessionem tuam ac sine mora tradi oportebit. Et quidem iidem Christiani non ea loca tantum, ad quae convenire consueverunt, sed alia etiam habuisse noscuntur, ad ius corporis eorum, id est Ecclesiarum, non hominum singulorum, pertinentia, ea omnia lege qua superius comprehendimus, citra ullam prorsus ambiguitatem vel controversiam hisdem Christianis, id est, corpori et conventiculis eorum reddi iubebis."—Lactantius, *De Mortibus Persecutorum,* c. 48—*MPL,* VII, 270.

[16] If the intention of Constantine had been actually to grant property rights to the Church it is hard to understand why he ordered all the property, even that which had passed into the hands of innocent owners, to be restored and why he ordained that those owners should be indemnified out of the public treasury.—*Cf.* Augustine, *Commentary on Canon Law,* vol. VI, *Administrative Law,* (2 ed., St. Louis: B. Herder Book Co., 1923), p. 552; De Rossi, *Roma sotteranea cristiana,* I, 104; Löning, *Geschichte des deutschen Kirchenrechts* (2 vols., Strassburg, 1878), I, 169.

[17] "Habeat unusquisque licentiam, sanctissimo Catholico venerabilique concilio decedens bonorum, quod optavit relinquere."—C.Th. (16.2) 4;

recognized in other religious societies.[18] This right was repeatedly confirmed,[19] and even though Theodosius II (408–450) issued three decrees which are apparently indirect violations of it,[20] it became an acknowledged right in Roman law.

The laws made by the Emperors Honorius (395–423) and Gratian (375–383) attest further to the fact that in the fourth and fifth centuries it was the usual policy of the civil government to acknowledge the right of the Church to acquire and hold property. These Emperors favored the Church either by ordering pagan temples to be turned over to it [21] or by commanding that property, taken from it by the Donatists, Priscillianists, and others, be restored to it as to its rightful owner.[22] Similar legislation was enacted under Theodosius I (379–395) and Valentinian III (425–455) against the Montanists.[23] Valentinian III in the West and Martian in the East confirmed all the legislation of their predecessors which acknowledged the rights of the Church and granted privileges to church property.[24] They directed that all bequests made to the poor should be held valid, and should be received and administered by the Church.[25]

The Emperors Leo and Anthemius revoked laws against the Church, recognized its rights, and restored all privileges previously granted by the Emperors.[26]

C (1.2) 1. Contrary to the assertion of Friedberg (*Lehrbuch des katholischen und evangelischen Kirchenrechts,* § 167) this was no mere privilege but a recognition of a right. The edict continues: "Nihil est quod magis hominibus debeatur, quam ut supremae voluntatis, postquam iam aliud velle non possunt, liber sit stilus et licitum quod iterum non redit arbitrium." *Cf.* also Carrière, *De Iustitia et Iure,* I, n. 99.

[18] "Collegium si nullo speciali privilegio subnixum est, hereditatem capere non posse dubium non est."—C (6.24) 8.

[19] C (1.2) 13—Valentinian III (425–455) and Martian (450–457); C (1.2) 14—Leo I (457–474) and Anthemius (467–472); C (1.2) 15—Zeno (474–491); C (1.3) 45—Justinian (527–565).

[20] C.Th. (16.2) 20, 22, 27. These laws forbade clerics and bishops to accept gifts or bequests from widows and orphans. They were justified as a necessary remedy for certain abuses.

[21] C.Th. (16.10) 20.

[22] C.Th. (16.6) 2; (16.5) 43.

[23] C.Th. (16.5) 52, 54, 57, 65.

[24] C (1.2) 12.

[25] C (1.3) 24; (1.2) 15.

[26] C (1.2) 16; (1.3) 34.

Justinian abolished many restrictions imposed by his predecessors on the right of the Church to acquire property, and provided further for the protection of the rights of the Church over all the property it held. In particular he provided for the property left by will to the Church or to pious foundations, sanctioned bequests to such pious causes as hospitals, relief of the poor, the redemption of captives and slaves, etc., and ordered the fulfilment of trusts, such as the payment of sums of money to a church or the erection of a hospital or oratory, within a certain time specified by law.[27] To safeguard the property of the Church he decreed that it could not be alienated.[28]

The right to acquire property was recognized in several other constitutions. When a person entered a monastery he was considered as offering his property to the monastery. The monastery could accept the property, which, once accepted, could not be alienated.[29] The property of priests, deacons, deaconesses, subdeacons, monks, and lower clerics who died intestate and left no heirs went to the church or monastery to which they had been attached.[30] One who defiantly ravished a virgin consecrated to God lost his property as a penalty; the property was acquired by the church to which the virgin was attached.[31] Donations to churches and other ecclesiastical corporations up to the value of fifty solidi were valid without a written contract; but a written document was required if the value of the property to be donated exceeded fifty solidi.[32] The Church, therefore, could acquire property by will, donation, or any "lucrative title." [33]

Under the Christian Emperors, then, the right to acquire and hold property was recognized and safeguarded by the civil law. Not only individual clerics and bishops, but individual churches as well could hold title to property. Moreover, privileges were granted to the property owned by the Church.[34] Thus the right to acquire property which had been exercised by the Church from the first century was recognized and safeguarded by the civil law.

27 C (1.2) 26; (1.3) 45, 49; N (131.9).
28 C (1.2) 21; N (7.12); (7.11).
29 N (5.5); (123.38).
30 C (1.3) 20.
31 C (1.3) 53.
32 C (1.2) 19.
33 C (1.2) 22; (1.3) 45.
34 C (1.2) 26.

C. The Right to Acquire in Canon Law

After the edict of Constantine the Church entered a period in which it could acquire both movable and immovable property publicly and freely. The adversaries of the Church's right to acquire property [85] claim that this was due to privileges granted the Church by the civil law. They view the edicts of the Emperors not as recognitions of the Church's native right, but as actual concessions of rights never possessed before. Such a view conflicts not only with the evident exercise of the right to acquire during centuries when the Church was not recognized by the civil law, but also with the actual state of affairs as manifested in the canon law of the period. At a time when the civil law afforded sufficient security for church rights the ecclesiastical legislators exhibit an independence and autonomy that bespeaks their consciousness of the independent rights of the Church. Independently of the civil law they legislate for the acquisition and administration of temporal goods, and brand interference with the property rights of the Church as a "sacrilege."

1. *Local Councils*

That the Church has the right to temporal goods which are to be used for pious purposes, and not for the personal comfort of their administrators, is clearly the intent of the Council of Ancyra (314) [86] and of the Council of Antioch (341).[87] Refusal to deliver to the Church property left to it by will was regarded as a serious violation of its rights, and as a sacrilege by the Council of Vaison (442).[88] The II Council of Arles (443) passed similar legislation asserting the right of the Church to acquire property.[89]

The interference of the laity with the property rights of the Church—acquisition as well as administration—was removed as a matter of principle from the earliest times. The III Synod of Rome (502) repudiated the constitution of Basilius, which limited

[85] *E. g.*, Friedberg, *Lehrbuch des katholischen und evangelischen Kirchenrechts*, § 167.

[86] Can. 15—Harduin, I, 327.

[87] Can. 24—Harduin, I, 603, 606.

[88] Can. 4—Harduin, I, 1788.

[89] Can. 47—Harduin, II, 777.

the power of the Church to administer its own property, expressly because laymen had no legislative rights in ecclesiastical matters. Such rights belonged exclusively to the Church for they "have been entrusted by God to the priests." [40]

The Council of Agde (506) presupposed the right of the Church to acquire property. Canon 6 declared that bishops to whom something had been given, not for themselves but for some pious cause, were not to regard the property so given as something personal or to use it for their own benefit. They were to consider it as having been given to the Church. Evidently it was understood in those early days that the Church was capable of acquiring temporal goods, and that ownership by the Church was something different from ownership by churchmen. The Fathers of Agde held that at least the individual churches—dioceses and parishes—had the right to possess property. They expressly stated that this right was to be safeguarded by those who managed the property.[41]

Many other councils also based legislation on the capacity and right of the Church and of individual moral persons within the Church to acquire and to possess. The I Council of Orleans (511) decreed that Church property was not subject to civil law prescription.[42]

In the fifth and six centuries local councils further made it clear that whatever property the Church possessed, it held in its own right independently of the temporal lord, who had no authority over it, nor any power to intervene in its administration. Thus the I Council of Orleans (511),[43] the Council of Clermont-Auvergne (535),[44] the Council of Lerida (546),[45] the III Council of Paris (557) [46] and the III and IV Councils of Toledo [47] made it clear that Church property was not subject to lay control. From the I Council of Orleans it is obvious that the Church had the right

[40] C. 1, D. XCVI; Thiel, *Epistolae Romanorum Pontificum Genuinae,* I (Brunsbergae, 1868), 687–689.

[41] Can. 6—Harduin, II, 998.

[42] Can. 23—Harduin, II, 1011.

[43] Can. 5—Harduin, II, 1009.

[44] Can. 5—Harduin, II, 1181.

[45] Cap. 3—c. 1, C. X, q. 1.

[46] Can. 1—Mansi, IX, 743.

[47] Can. 19—c. 2, C. X, q. 1; can. 32—c. 6, C. X, q. 1; Harduin, III, 482, 587.

to own and administer realty, and that this right was exercised independently of even those who had donated the property. The right to acquire was further established by the II Council of Lyons (567) [48] and the Council of Valence (584).[49]

Thus by the sixth century one finds the Church asserting a right that is not denied or questioned—a right that does not come from the civil law (for its exercise does not depend upon the civil law), but from some source above the civil law.[50]

An ingenuous acknowledgment of the Church's right regarding property was made by King Wihtred of Kent about 696. His words show that the Church had made claims to the right to acquire and possess its property free from interference by the court or civil power. He says that he has "learned from the institutions of our forefathers that no layman ought with right to appropriate to himself a Church or any of the things which to a Church belong." In consequence of this teaching he declares that no church property is to be disturbed with any claims of lordship. "And therefore strongly and faithfully we appoint and decree, and in the name of Almighty God, and of all the saints we forbid to all kings our successors, and to all ealdormen, and to all laymen, ever any lordship over churches and over any of their possessions which I or my predecessors in days of old have given for the glory of Christ, and our Lady St. Mary and the Holy Apostles." [51]

The Council of Lessines in 743 found it necessary to safeguard church property that had been given to laymen by *precaria*. The institution of *precaria* by which princes bestowed on their lay servants revenues of churches, monasteries, etc., was really secularization of church property. Although the *dominium* of the property remained with the Church, the *dominium utile* was transferred at the request (*preces*) of the king or prince to the layman, and was very apt to pass on to his heirs.[52] The Council of Meaux (845)

[48] Can. 2—Harduin, III, 354.

[49] *Cf.* Harduin, III, 457.

[50] Although not mentioned in the decrees, the source of church property rights is hinted at by the Council of Vaison (442) in canon 4 when it states: "Amico quippiam rapere furtum est, ecclesiam fraudare sacrilegium."—Harduin, I, 1788.

[51] Haddan and Stubbs, *Councils and Ecclesiastical Documents relating to Great Britain and Ireland* (3 vols., Oxford, 1869–1873), III, 244.

[52] Can. 2—Harduin, III, 1921.

had to decree that no power could force one to grant lands or other church property in *precaria,*[53] and that he who took property from a moral person within the Church was guilty not only of theft but of sacrilege and was bound to restitution.[54]

The Councils of Aix (816),[55] Paris (829)[56] and Trosly (909)[57] further established the right of the Church to property. One who violated that right by stealing the property of the Church was guilty of sacrilege.

Gregory VII (1073–1085) asserted the right and ability of ecclesiastical juridical persons to acquire and own in the Roman synod of 1078. Other councils, for example that of Toulouse in 1119,[58] issued similar legislation. Such legislation could only come from a corporate body that was conscious of its own independent right to acquire temporal goods.

2. *General Councils*

The I Council of Constantinople (381) was concerned with the proper administration of Church possessions and provided that churches and church property be administered by the bishops.[59] The Council of Chalcedon (451) attests to the exercise of the right to acquire property,[60] and legislated to protect church property during the vacancy of benefices[61] and to prevent its conversion to secular uses.[62]

The II Council of Nicaea (787) reaffirmed the legislation of the six previous councils (canon 1), and provided for the better administration of church property.[63]

The IV Council of Constantinople (869–870) distinguished between church property and the property of churchmen and legislated

[53] Can. 22—Mansi, XIV, 823; Harduin, IV, 1486.

[54] Anselm of Lucca, *Collectio Canonum* (Ed. Thaner, Innsbruck, 1906–1915), Lib. V, c. 36; Harduin, IV, 1493.

[55] Can. 116—Harduin, IV, 1132.

[56] Cap. 15—Harduin, IV, 1307-1309.

[57] Cap. 4—Harduin, VI, 513–515.

[58] Can. 4, 6—Harduin, VII, 1979.

[59] Can. 2, 6—Harduin, I, 808–811.

[60] Can. 4—Harduin, II, 601, 604.

[61] Can. 22—Harduin, II, 609.

[62] Can. 24, 26—Harduin, II, 612.

[63] Can. 11, 12, 13—Harduin, IV, 494–495.

concerning the proper administration of the former. The independence of church property was asserted in canon 18, which decreed that no secular person could take away property that had been possessed by the Church for a period of thirty years, even though the Church could show no transfer of title.[64]

Up to the end of the eleventh century the legislation regarding lay interference with church ownership and administration had come from local councils and synods. The I Lateran Council (1123) provided the first instance of a general ecclesiastical law establishing the principle of the independent character of the Church's right regarding property. The doctrine of the Council was not new. Canon 4 repeated the teaching—even the very words—of local councils and synods held centuries before. But its importance lay in the fact that it was the first general or universal law on the subject. The Council in canon 4 said: "In accordance with the decision of Pope Stephen[65] we declare that lay persons, no matter how devout they may be, have no power to dispose of anything belonging to the Church, but according to the canons of the Apostles the supervision of all ecclesiastical affairs belongs to the bishop, who shall administer them comformably to the will of God. If, therefore, any prince or other layman shall arrogate to himself the disposition, control, or ownership of Church goods or property, let him be judged guilty of sacrilege."[66]

This canon together with other legislation of the Lateran Council ended the long strife over investiture. Like similar provisions of the Concordat of Worms of the year before,[67] the legislation of the Council insisted that the rights of the Church regarding property had not been conferred on it by any civil magistrate or prince, but belonged to it by right.

The doctrine of canon 4 was proclaimed anew by the II (1139) and III (1179) Lateran Councils in canons 25 and 14 respectively.[68] The II Lateran Council also widened the scope of the legislation of the Council of Chalcedon regarding the conservation

[64] Can. 15, 18—Harduin, V, 905, 907.

[65] This is a reference to the pseudo-Isidorian ordinances. *Cf.* Mansi, I, 892.

[66] *Fontes,* n. 7; Mansi, XXI, 282; English translation by Schroeder, *Disciplinary Decrees of the General Councils,* p. 180.

[67] *Cf.* Nussi, *Conventiones de Rebus Ecclesiasticis* (Mainz, 1870), p. 1.

[68] Mansi, XXI, 532; XXII, 225.

of church property during vacancies of episcopal sees. The Council of Chalcedon forbade clerics to seize church property; the II Council of the Lateran extended the prohibition to include laymen also.[69]

The General Councils regarded property as necessary for the Church and forbade its alienation. They decreed that property should be administered by the authority of the bishop. Laymen, even if sovereign rulers, had no authority over the administration and disposition of church property. The decrees of these councils exhibit the perfectly sovereign attitude of the Church concerning the acquisition, possession and administration of property. They manifest a consciousness of the right of the Church to own property. The councils in legislating as they did based their decrees upon the recognized right of the Church.

3. *Eleventh Century Collections of Law*

The collection of Burchard of Worms (+1025) [70] appeared early in the eleventh century in Western Germany. It illustrates the independence of the Church's right to property, and asserts the right of the Church to possess temporal goods without molestation by secular princes.[71]

The legislation gathered in the collection of Anselm of Lucca (+1086) [72] asserts the right of the Church to have property [73] and maintains the independence of the Church from interference by secular powers.[74] The solutions of cases indicate that the right of the Church to acquire and possess property derives from a source higher than the civil law.[75]

The *Decretum* of Ivo of Chartres (+1116),[76] which appeared

[69] Can. 5—Harduin, VII, 1208.

[70] *Decretum Burchardi* (circa 1008-1012)—*MPL,* CXL, 537 ff.

[71] *Decretum Burchardi,* Lib. III, cc. 6, 7, 8, 35, 36.

[72] Anselmi Lucensis *Collectio Canonum* (c. 1083).

[73] *Collectio Canonum,* Lib. IV, cc. 37, 44.

[74] "Non licet laico statuendi in Ecclesia praeter Romanum Pontificem habere aliquam potestatem; non placuit laicum statuendi in ecclesia habere aliquam potestatem, cui subsequendi manet necessitas non auctoritas imperandi; laicis quamvis religiosis nulla de ecclesiasticis facultatibus aliquid disponendi legitur unquam attributa facultas."—*Collectio Canonum,* Lib. V, cc. 8–10.

[75] *Collectio Canonum,* Lib. V, cc. 27, 33, 36, 45, 52.

[76] *Decretum Ivonis* (1095)—*MPL,* CLXI, 9 ff.

toward the end of the eleventh century, contains substantially the same legislation regarding the possession and administration of church property. Pastors and bishops were warned against selling to others or appropriating for themselves lands and possessions that belonged to their benefices.[77] Invaders and usurpers of church property were not to be admitted to communion.[78] Ivo then proceeded to discuss the doctrine of ownership. Earthly possessions were not lawfully held except by some title acquired from either divine or human law. He merely intimated that church property was held not by virtue of any concession of the civil magistrates but by natural right.[79]

From these collections it is seen that there existed in the eleventh century a well evolved concept of a juridical personality capable of possessing and acquiring property, yet separate from the personality of the administrator (pastor or bishop). In other words, the doctrine at this time regarding the Church's capacity to acquire property is characterized by: 1) an acknowledgment of the capacity to possess—this was mainly in regard to juridical persons within the Church; the juridical capacity of the Church itself to possess property had not yet been questioned, and hence there had been no occasion for a statement of doctrine on this point—2) the insistence that this right to acquire and possess be exercised with complete independence of all lay control. Since neither civil law nor civil rulers constituted the source from which the Church of Christ enjoyed the rights to acquire and to own, they had no power to dispose of the property that had been acquired.

4. *Gratian and the Decretals*

At the time of the *Decretum Gratiani* (c. 1140) the Church's right to possess property was so certainly acknowledged that the legislation of the *Decretum* concerns itself chiefly with secondary questions which arose out of the indubitable property rights of the Church. There is no express declaration that the Church has the capacity to acquire and possess temporal goods, such as there is in the present Code of Canon Law. Furthermore the *Decretum*

[77] *Decretum,* Lib. III, cc. 161, 166, 169.

[78] *Decretum,* Lib. III, c. 182. Ivo here quotes the III synod of Rome (502) held under Pope Symmachus.

[79] *Decretum,* Lib. III, c. 179.

Gratiani and the Decretals rarely speak of the possessions of the Church; their legislation concerns the possessions of individual churches, monasteries, benefices, etc. In other words, the subject of ownership as seen in the *Corpus Iuris Canonici* is more often a moral person within the Church than the Church itself. Yet the legislation regarding the individual churches is based on the higher right of the Church to have property.

It is clear that churches did possess the right to acquire property. They could accept gifts from the faithful,[80] and succeed to the property of clerics who died intestate.[81] There is a clear distinction made between the property that belonged to the church and that of the individual clerics. Bishops had to keep separate records of their own and of their church's property. These records were to be open to those whose duty it was to look after the welfare of the property.[82] Bishops could not alienate the property of the church, but could do what they pleased with their own possessions.[83] The church property in the diocese was to be in the hands of the bishop. He alone was to manage it. This meant that the church building and all endowments were under his control, and were to be administered according to his judgment.[84]

No lay authority could exercise any administrative power in church property or demand the distribution of church goods.[85] The churches and everything that belonged to them were exclusively under the control of the ecclesiastical authorities, and were altogether immune from lay interference.[86]

In their comments on the *Decretum Gratiani* the Glossators made much of the fact that lay rulers had no authority to dispose of church property. The decrees of lay princes had no effect when ecclesiastical possessions were concerned, for laymen had no powers over such property.[87] The Church owned property in its own

[80] C. 16, C. XII, q. 1; cc. 6, 13, 14, C. X, q. 1.

[81] C. 5, C. XIII, q. 5.

[82] *Dictum Gratiani*, c. 24, C. XII, q. 1; also cc. 19, 20, 21, C. XII, q. 1.

[83] C. XII, q. 2, *cf. Dictum Gratiani;* c. 5, X, *de rebus ecclesiae alienandis vel non,* III, 13.

[84] C. 2, C. X, q. 1; c. 5, C. X, q. 1.

[85] C. 6, C. X, q. 1; c. 59, C. XVI, q. 1.

[86] *Dictum Gratiani* at end of C. X, q. 1.

[87] Gloss to c. 1, D. XCVI, ad verbum *Illud autem;* also ad verbum *Casus.*

right. Moreover, it held that the civil power was bound to recognize its rights.[88]

The doctrine of the Decretals is the same. The Church had the capacity to possess and become the owner of property.[89] It enjoyed the rights of a minor, so that if it suffered injury through the alienation of some piece of property it would have the right to have the property restored.[90] Church property, even though not consecrated, enjoyed immunity [91] and was entirely free from all lay control. The principle, "Laicis etiam religiosis super ecclesiis et personis ecclesiasticis nulla sit attributa facultas," was frequently invoked. Pope Innocent III (1198–1216) used it to settle a case involving church property in 1199,[92] and the IV Lateran Council invoked it against the secular princes in 1215.[93]

The Church possessed its property with complete independence from the civil authority. Its capacity and right were not derived from the king or emperor, but belonged to it by inherent right and the will of its Divine Founder. No layman, then, no matter how devout or powerful, be he the king himself, had any voice in the administration of church property. Nor could a lay monarch limit the extent of church possessions or confer church property upon one of his subjects.[94] Church possession was based on a right wholly outside the sphere of his jurisdiction. Once property came into the possession of the Church it passed from the jurisdiction of laymen, and was to be ruled and administered according to ecclesiastical law,[95] and no secular authority could force grants (*precaria*) of church property to be made to individuals.[96]

Ecclesiastical legislation, therefore, both local and general, recognized and defended the inherent capacity and right of the Church to acquire temporal goods. The defense and vindication of the right of the Church (as distinct from individual bodies within the Church) was necessarily more implicit than explicit, because dur-

[88] C. 21, 22, C. XXIII, q. 8.
[89] C. 2, X, *de consuetudine,* I, 4.
[90] C. 1, X, *de in integrum restitutione,* I, 41.
[91] C. 9, X, *de immunitate ecclesiarum,* III, 49.
[92] C. 10, X, *de constitutionibus,* I, 2.
[93] C. 12, X, *de rebus ecclesiae alienandis vel non,* III, 13.
[94] C. 2, X, *de rebus ecclesiae alienandis vel non,* III, 13.
[95] C. 1, 2, 5, 6, 14, C. X, q. 1.
[96] C. 4, C. X, q. 2.

ing the first twelve centuries of the Church's existence that right was never called in question.

D. Vindication of the Right to Acquire against Mortmain Statutes

The mortmain laws were never accepted in principle by the Church authorities. It is true that the matter in question was only the limitation of the Church's right to acquire, and not the denial of that right. Still the Popes opposed the statutes with all their authority. They maintained that all such laws were without vigor since the civil legislator had no competence over ecclesiastical affairs. It is noteworthy that the Popes and the papal pronouncements in this connection do not stress the right of the Church to acquire property—a right that was not at all denied—but confine themselves strictly to the matter in question, the unlawful limitation of church rights by civil authorities.

Alexander III (1159–1181) inveighed against the almost total subordination of Church funds and property to the interests of the princes and lords, and prohibited under pain of excommunication "those who seem to have power" from presuming to repeat their demands. The Church, he claimed, must be allowed free exercise of its right to administer its property. Church property could be taxed only with the consent of the ecclesiastical authorities.[97]

Alexander IV (1254–1261), exasperated by the insolence of the officials of the French king who had repeatedly violated the rights and privileges of church possessions in France, sought to end the forced alienations of church property by a restatement of church law and a threat of penalties.[98] In order to restore the

[97] C. 4, X, *De immunitate ecclesiarum, cemeterii, et rerum ad eas pertinentium,* III, 49.

[98] It seems that the authorities, local as well as royal, had given ecclesiastics the choice either of paying the assessments imposed on property acquired by religious corporations, or of handing ownership over to some other person who would pay. Since clergymen were forbidden by canon law to pay taxes on church property (they were liable to taxes on their private possessions and in times of public need they never refused to share the common burden by the offering of donations), this ruling really amounted to secularization of property. It was more than alienation, for it seems that the Church received no consideration for such transfers of her property.—*Cf.* glosses to c. 1, *de immunitate ecclesiarum,* III, 23, in VI°.

Church to the enjoyment of its full rights and liberty and to eliminate the abuses, Alexander IV decreed that the mortmain tax was unlawful and that no temporal power had the right to force churches or clergymen to sell, alienate, or otherwise transfer ownership of church possessions, or even to limit the amount of property that could be acquired by the Church.[99]

The law of Alexander IV is much stronger than the constitution of Alexander III. The earlier document permitted church property to be taxed if the bishops judged the taxes to be necessary for the common welfare, but the constitution of Alexander IV is not modified by any such exception. Under no circumstances were merely civil authorities to limit the rights of the Church to acquire temporal goods. Alexander IV's constitution is the most outspoken statement of Church rights up to his time. Even though it is placed in the Decretals of Boniface VIII under the title *De immunitate,* its doctrine is based not on privilege but on the inherent capacity and right of the Church. There is no appeal to concessions granted by the civil power, or to violated promises made by temporal princes. Instead, the Pope invokes his apostolic authority by which he has the care and guardianship of all the churches, and forbids further violations of the native or inherent right of the Church to temporal possessions, and to liberty in their acquisition and ownership.

Boniface VIII (1294–1303) protested again against the continuation of the abuses repeatedly condemned by his predecessors. In his decretal, *"Clericis laicos,"* [100] he reminded lay rulers "that all power over the clergy, over persons and the property of the Church is denied to them." In another constitution he struck at the attempts to prevent the Church from acquiring temporal possessions.[101] As the ecclesiastical bodies continued, in spite of the mortmain laws, to hold on to their property, the civil authorities claimed the right to tax them. If they refused both to give up ownership and to pay the taxes, the authorities proposed to lay a sort of civil excommunication or boycott on them, and actually forbade their subjects to have any civil or commercial relations with them. It was hoped that these measures would in time force

[99] C. 1, *de immunitate ecclesiarum,* III, 23, in VI°.
[100] C. 3, *de immunitate ecclesiarum,* III, 23, in VI°.
[101] C. 5, *de immunitate ecclesiarum,* III, 23, in VI°.

the clergy to agree to the encroachments of the civil power on the rights of the Church. Boniface VIII, when he was advised of this, hurled a more powerful excommunication at the civil authorities. "We decree," he said, "that if temporal princes at any time forbid their subjects to sell anything to prelates, clergymen, or other ecclesiastical persons . . . or to render them any other services, they are *eo ipso* excommunicated, since they have presumed to act thus in order to restrict the liberty of the Church." [102]

In spite of these repeated efforts and protests of the Popes the mortmain laws either continued in force or were revived from time to time. The Holy See seems to have been acutely aware of them after the days of Boniface VIII. In the concordat between Alfonse V of Aragon and the bishops (which later was confirmed by Nicholas V in 1451) the Church obtained a revocation of mortmain laws,[103] and similarly in the concordat with Naples in 1741 under Benedict XIV[104] provision had to be made for church property that, according to civil statutes, was subject to taxation because of mortmain laws.

The unchanging attitude and teaching of the Holy See has ever been: 1) that the laws of mortmain are in themselves unjust and have ever been hostile to the interests of the Church, and 2) that because of the lack of jurisdiction such laws issued by the civil power are null and void unless they have been specially condoned by the Roman Pontiff in a concordat with the government.

E. Vindication of the Right to Acquire against Heretical Doctrines

The denial of the right of the Church to acquire temporal goods by the fanatical sects (Waldenses, Albigenses, Fraticelli, and Wycliffites, Lombards)[105] and by the political philosophers (John of Jandun and Marsilius of Padua)[106] was condemned by Popes and Councils. The errors of the Waldenses and the Albigenses were repeatedly condemned throughout the eleventh and twelfth

[102] C. 5, *de immunitate ecclesiarum,* III, 23, in VI°.

[103] Mercati, *Raccolta,* p. 189.

[104] *Ibid.,* p. 339.

[105] *Cf. supra,* pp. 13 ff.

[106] *Cf. supra,* p. 40.

centuries.[107] In the fourteenth century the teachings of the Fraticelli were proscribed. John XXII (1316–1334) condemned the doctrine that "there are two churches, one carnal and rich which is the Roman Church, the other spiritual and poor which is that of the Fraticelli." [108] This condemnation of the Fraticelli implicitly asserted the right of the Church to own property, for it taught that the ownership of property by the Church was not contrary to the precepts of Christ. The Pope declared that Christ and His Apostles not only used temporal goods, but actually owned them. Hence, the Church was but following His example in vindicating for the clergy the right to acquire temporal goods.[109]

This same Pope appointed a commission to investigate the teachings of Marsilius of Padua. The commission examined his work, *Defensor Pacis,* from which it took five propositions. The first is pertinent here: "These reprobates (*i. e.,* Marsilius and John of Jandun) do not hesitate to affirm in what is related of Christ in the gospel of St. Matthew, viz., that He paid tribute . . . that He did so not through condescension and liberality, but of necessity—an assertion that runs counter to the teaching of the Gospel and the words of our Savior. If one were to believe these men, it would follow that all property of the Church belongs to the emperor and that he may take possession of it again as his own." [110] Following the recommendations of the commission the Pope in a bull, *"Licet iuxta doctrinam,"* condemned Marsilius as a heretic and his doctrines as "contrary to Scripture and hostile to the Catholic faith, heretical, and erroneous." [111]

[107] Council of Rheims (1049), Acta diei tertii (post canones)—Harduin, VI, 1007; Council of Toulouse (1119), can. 3—Harduin, VII, 1978–1979; III Lateran Council (1179), can. 27—Harduin, VII, 1683; Lucius III, const., *"Ad abolendum diversarum"*—Mansi, XXII, 476; Innocent III, const., *"Eius exemplo"*—*Denz.* nn. 420, 427.

Admarus in his chronicle mentions that the Council of Charroux (1028) condemned the Albigenses—Harduin, VI, 843.

[108] Const., *"Gloriosam Ecclesiam,"* 23 ian. 1318—*Denz.* n. 485.

[109] Const., *"Cum inter nonnullos,"* 13 nov. 1323—*Denz.* n. 494; c. 4, *de Verborum Significatione,* tit. XIV, in Extravag. Joan. XXII. Joannes Marius in his *Liber de schismatibus et concil.,* cap. 1, mentions that the Council of Avignon (1327) condemned the Fraticelli—Harduin, VIII, 1537.

[110] Translation by Salembier in *Catholic Encyclopedia,* s.v. "Marsilius of Padua."

[111] *Denz.* nn. 495, 500; *cf.* also Scheys, *De Iure Ecclesiae Acquirendi et Possidendi,* 163; *Coll. Lac.,* VII, 629, note 3.

The errors of Wycliffe's teaching were recognized and condemned by the English bishops, and later by Pope Martin V (1417–1431). The Council of London (1382) drew up a list of twenty-four articles held by Wycliffe. They condemned as heretical the teaching: "It is contrary to Sacred Scripture for churchmen to have temporal possessions." [112] The doctrine of ownership founded on grace was condemned as erroneous, as was the teaching that the temporal lords could take away church property because of the sins of the churchmen.[113] The tenor of the articles condemned by the Council of London was incorporated by Pope Martin V into his constitutions *"Inter cunctas"* and *"In eminentis"* [114] which solemnly condemned Wycliffe's errors.

Against Wycliffe's contention that clerics should live a life of evangelical poverty and not hold property either in their own name or in the name of the Church, Martin V condemned the proposition on which that contention was based: "Contra scripturam sacram est quod viri ecclesiastici habeant possessiones." [115] Censuring the more fundamental error, the Pope condemned Wycliffe's doctrine of ownership founded on grace. Article 15 stated in effect that a man in mortal sin was not really a civil lord, a prelate, or a bishop.[116] Articles 16 and 18 further declared untenable the teaching that flowed as a consequence from that erroneous doctrine of ownership. Article 16 repudiated the assertion that temporal lords could arbitrarily take property from the Church merely because the Church's ministers were habitually delinquent. In Article 18 the Pope asserted that the Church's right to tithes did not depend on the conduct of her ministers.[117] Moreover, in Article 36 he denied that the Popes and the bishops who owned property were heretics. Therefore, secular princes did not sin by granting temporal goods to the Church, nor the Popes or clerics in receiving them.[118]

To prevent the spread of the condemned teachings the Pope decreed that all who were suspected of believing or of teaching

[112] Concl. 10—Harduin, VIII, 1891.

[113] Concl. 6, 7—Harduin, VIII, 1891.

[114] *Fontes,* n. 43; *Denz.* nn. 581–625.

[115] Art. 10—*Fontes,* n. 43; *Denz.* n. 590.

[116] "Nullus est dominus civilis, nullus est praelatus, nullus est episcopus, dum est in peccato mortali."—*Fontes,* n. 43; *Denz.* n. 595.

[117] *Fontes,* n. 43; *Denz.* nn. 596, 598.

[118] *Fontes,* n. 43; *Denz.* nn. 613, 616, 619.

these doctrines were to be questioned as to their belief. The tenor of the questions was set forth in the constitution, *"Inter cunctas,"* of February 22, 1418, as follows: "Utrum credat quod liceat personis Ecclesiasticis absque peccato huius mundi habere possessiones et bona temporalia. Item, utrum credat quod laicis ipsa ab eis auferre potestate propria non liceat, immo quod sic auferentes, tollentes, et invadentes bona ipsa Ecclesiastica sint tamquam sacrilegi puniendi, etiamsi male viverent personae Ecclesiasticae bona huiusmodi possidentes. Item, utrum credat quod huiusmodi ablatio et invasio cuicumque sacerdoti, etiam male viventi, temere vel violenter facta, vel illata, inducant sacrilegium." [119]

In response, therefore, to the errors of Wycliffe's teachings the Pope issued a condemnation of the false doctrine in which he implied the right of the Church to acquire and own property independently of the temporal lords, and denied that any person was authorized by any law to seize or expropriate church property. The Pope's defense of the proprietary rights of the Church was limited to those points that were denied by Wycliffe; he did not give a detailed exposition of Church rights, nor did he expand the arguments on which they were based.

F. Vindication of the Right to Acquire against Violations by the Secular Powers

The teaching that it had thus constantly proclaimed and sanctioned the Church sought to have recognized by the civil governments. In the agreement between Alfonse V of Aragon (1416–1458) and the bishops, which was later confirmed by Pope Nicholas V (1447–1455), the king approved and confirmed whatever alienations or transfers of property had been made in favor of churches or ecclesiastics and acknowledged the rights of the Church over such property by revoking the mortmain levy that hitherto had been imposed on property acquired by the Church. He recognized the freedom of the Church to acquire temporal goods, "ita ut ecclesiae et aliae personae ecclesiasticae loca pia et religiosa acquirentes . . . non teneantur propterea ad aliquod ius mortizacionis . . . solvendum." [120] In this case the native rights of the

[119] *Fontes,* n. 43; *Denz.* nn. 684–686.

[120] Mercati, *Raccolta,* p. 189.

Church were safeguarded. The concordat removed the illegitimate restrictions placed on the exercise of the right to acquire and to possess.

The V Lateran Council (1512–1517) forbade secular princes to seize or hold the income of churches, monasteries, and benefices. It decreed also that no civil authority was to hinder the beneficiary from obtaining possession of the fruits of his benefice. The Council based its legislation on principles of public law, *viz.*, that the full administration and management of all ecclesiastical incomes belong to the ecclesiastical authority, and that divine law forbids secular rulers to interfere in the disposition of church property. Evidently the Council recognized that the Church possessed its property in virtue of its divine constitution as a perfect society and not because of the concessions of the State.[121]

In spite of the efforts of the Popes and the bishops, the Church's claim to acquire and possess property free from civil interference was not universally acknowledged. It had been seriously violated in France, as the stipulations of the bull "*Primitiva illa*" (1516) indicate.[122] In order to safeguard the spiritual jurisdiction of the Church Pope Leo X (1513–1521) deemed it prudent to surrender to the French government practically all control of the temporal possessions of the Church. The agreement of 1516 appears to recognize the theory of church ownership, yet it gives to the civil power the appointment of almost all the administrators of church property.[123] The right to own property was not questioned; but its free administration was seriously impaired. From contemporary accounts it appears that the cupidity of many civil rulers was stirred by the considerable amount of land owned by the Church in the years immediately preceding the Protestant Revolt.[124]

The teachings of Wycliffe seem to have induced some to confiscate church property because of the crimes or supposed crimes

[121] Leo X, const., "*Supernae dispositionis,*" 5 maii 1514, § 39—*Fontes,* n. 65.

[122] Nussi, *Conventiones,* pp. 20–35.

[123] Nussi, *Conventiones,* pp. 20–29; Mercati, *Raccolta,* pp. 233–241.

[124] Certainly the possessions of the Church were extensive enough to arouse an anti-clerical feeling among the laity. A letter attributed to the noted scholar Jerome Aleander (circa 1541) urged, as one of the reasons for holding a general council, the hostile attitude of the laity due to the size of the possessions of the Church.—*Concilium Tridentinum* (Editio Goerresiana), XII, pars 1, 353. *Cf.* also introductory note, *ibid.,* p. 342.

committed by the clergymen who administered it. The civil authorities in places claimed a right to the ownership of tithes and first fruits which by law were to be dedicated to the uses of the Church. They appropriated churches and other ecclesiastical possessions in the cities and villages. They urged that church property was no different from property owned by their own subjects, but was to be acquired and held in accordance with the civil law.[125]

The heretical doctrines of the sixteenth century incited the enemies of the Church to take advantage of political disturbances to despoil the Church of its possessions.[126] The right of the Church to acquire had been limited by the mortmain laws; now the right to possess was flagrantly violated by these usurpations. Even in a general congregation of the Council of Trent the representative of his "Most Christian Majesty" the King of France, had the temerity to declare that the property of the Church in France was subject to the king and could be used, if necessity warranted, for the purposes of the State.[127] Some civil rulers, at least, sought legal justification for their control and seizure of ecclesiastical incomes by alleging the superior rights of the State.[128]

While preparations were being made for the convocation of the Council of Trent Pope Paul III (1534–1549) in a bull, *"Superni dispositione"* (Jan. 1542?), which he delivered to a number of the Cardinals but which he never promulgated, asserted that the Church has the right to acquire and own temporal goods, because without

[125] For a list of abuses committed by civil authorities see the accounts of Benedict de Nobile, and Frederick Nausea in *Concilium Tridentinum,* XII, pars 1, 579, 583, 369.

[126] "Contra tam humana quam divina, tamque ecclesiastica quam civilia iura eam intulerunt violentiam, ut eos sc. clericos de possessionibus eorum protruserint nec parum multa monasteria templa sacerdotiaque partim spoliaverint et occupaverint partim destruxerint."—*Concilium Tridentinum,* XII, pars 1, 369.

[127] See the speech of Rainaldus Ferrerius, Sept. 22, 1563—*Concilium Tridentinum,* IX, 843. Ferrerius was suspected of heresy even before his speech. Later he joined Henry of Navarre and Calvin and publicly espoused their cause.—*Ibid.*

[128] *Cf. op. cit.,* IX, 1053.—An indication of the times is to be seen in the recommendation of one bishop in the Council who advised against the Council's declaring that the bishops were merely *dispensatores* of church property and revenues, lest the lay rulers seize upon the word as a loophole to justify seizure of all church property.

them it cannot fulfill its spiritual mission. He exhorted all those in power to observe and respect the Church's right. The Emperor and all kings, princes, and other civil rulers, even parliaments and legislative bodies, were warned to be content with those possessions to which they had a right, and not to seek those which belong to others. They were not to intrude themselves in matters that came under ecclesiastical jurisdiction. Nor were they to tax ecclesiastical goods or to appropriate to themselves either tithes or any other church property. They were not to molest ecclesiastical holdings, but instead they were to assist the bishops, carrying out their wishes and extending to them the aid of the secular arm in the restoration of illegally appropriated goods.[129]

The canons of the Council added sanctions to these decrees by inflicting penalties on all violators. Anyone who dared to turn church holdings to his own profit, or to usurp ecclesiastical property would fall under excommunication until he had returned that which he had taken. The same penalty applied to those who impeded the payment or receipt of the revenues due to churchmen from church property.[130]

In Session XXV, *de ref.*, the Council dealt with those who strove to appropriate the tithes that were due to the Church. Various means had been used to violate the right of the Church in this matter. Not only were the tithes directly taken by those who had no right to them, but sometimes pressure was employed by these persons to prevent the payment of tithes by those who were under obligation to pay them. The Council declared that all such methods constituted an *"invasio rerum alienarum."* It ordered the payment of the tithes for the future and excommunicated all who withheld or prevented payment. Absolution could not be had before a full restitution had been made.[131]

While the Council did not explicitly mention the inherent right of the Church, the legislation referred to above has been understood and interpreted as a vindication and a protection of that

[129] N. 44—*Concilium Tridentinum,* IV, 496.

[130] *Concilium Tridentinum,* Sess. XXII, *de ref.,* c. 11. A comparison of the text as it was finally adopted with the text as originally proposed will show how the Fathers of the Council wished to protect all ecclesiastical property. *Cf.* c. 14—*Concilium Tridentinum,* VIII, 926.

[131] *Conc. Trid.,* Sess. XXV, *de ref.,* c. 12.

right.[182] The penalties inflicted by the Council were not the result of the political, civil and spiritual unrest of the times, nor was it their exclusive purpose to safeguard the prosecution of the merely temporal welfare of the Church.[183] The property which the Council of Trent sought to protect comprised the goods set apart and consecrated to God: *res Dei, patrimonium Christi.*[184] Such property had always been regarded as the special property of the Church to which it had a natural right. For it was such property that enabled the Church to fulfill its mission.[185] Moreover, the Council provided that when an ecclesiastical establishment ceased to exist, or when its income was too small for its needs, its property was to be joined to that of some neighboring establishment.[186] It was never to pass to the State, therefore; for it was not subject to the civil laws.

G. Recognition of the Right to Acquire by the Secular Powers

From the determined but isolated attempts of civil rulers to restrict the acquisition of property by ecclesiastical institutions, which Alexander III and Boniface VIII so strenuously opposed, the dependence of ecclesiastical institutions upon the civil power was, in the seventeenth, eighteenth, and nineteenth centuries, gradually erected into a system. In the days of Alexander III and Boniface VIII the existence of religious corporations was not threatened; it was only their right to acquire property that was limited. In the centuries following the Protestant Revolt the prohibition to acquire property became stricter and finally the approval and authorization of the civil power was required for the founding of every religious corporation and establishment.

[182] Moulart, *L'Eglise et L'Etat,* 563; Scheys, *De Iure Ecclesiae Acquirendi et possidendi,* 165; Michiels, *Principia Generalia de Personis* (Lublin, 1932), p. 365; Ottaviani, *Institutiones Iuris Publici Ecclesiastici,* I, n. 201.

[183] *Cf.* Pius IX Encycl., *"Quanta cura,"* 8 dec. 1864—*Fontes,* n. 542; *Denz.* 1697.

[184] Sess. XXV, *de ref.*, cap. 1.

[185] Tertullian, *Apologeticus,* cap. 39—*MPL,* I, 535; Augustine, *In Ioannis Evangelium,* tract. 50, 52—*MPL,* XXV, 1762, 1803; Scheys, *op. cit.*, p. 165; Moulart, *op. cit.*, p. 563.

[186] Sess. XXI, *de ref.*, c. 7.

The doctrine that the Catholic Church had no right to acquire property unless the State gave its permission was a logical deduction from the tenets of Richerianism and Febronianism.[187] The legal basis for this teaching was the concept that the Church received its juridical personality from the civil law of the land. As this doctrine spread and as its effects became apparent it was met by the insistent teaching of the ecclesiastical authorities that the Catholic Church by its very nature was a perfect society and thus possessed a legitimate and natural right to property. Local councils and concordats between the Holy See and various governments clarified and made more effective the Catholic doctrine, emphatically insisting upon the inherent character of the right to acquire and its complete independence from the State.

France.—In France the excesses following the Revolution were responsible for the spoliation of the property of the Church. Confronted with an almost completely empty treasury, the liberal statesmen invoked their favorite principle that the government has the right to suppress any foundation for reasons of public utility. Secularization was decreed by law. Lands, churches, buildings were taken over. But in 1801 when the new government came to an agreement with the Holy See the difficulties over church property were composed. The number of dioceses in the new republic was reduced, which, no doubt, meant that the Church surrendered a goodly portion of its holdings (Art. 3). Those who during the revolution had acquired church property without just title were not to be disturbed; the Church agreed to condone their usurpations (Art. 13). On the other hand the French government promised the bishops and the parish priests a suitable maintenance (Art. 14). The churches that had not been alienated and were necessary for worship were to be put "at the disposition of the bishops" (Art. 12). It was further stipulated that the government would allow Catholics freedom to endow the Church with new funds "if such should be agreeable" (Art. 15).[188] From this it can be seen that, although the concordat contains no statement of the rights enjoyed by the Church, a studious effort was made to preserve these rights

[187] Cf. Tarquini, *Iuris Ecclesiastici Publici Institutiones* (Romae, 1875), II, 7; Zaccaria, *Anti-febronius* (5 vols., Bruxellis, 1829), IV, 165–167.

[188] Nussi, *Conventiones,* pp. 140–141.

in practice insofar as was possible. The right to possess and to acquire was maintained even though the Church did not insist on the return of all its property.

A few years later, when the monarchy was restored, there was drawn up a new concordat which abrogated that of 1801 and revived the agreement of 1516 between Pope Leo X and King Francis I.[139] The new concordat restored the churches that had been suppressed in 1801 (Art. 4); it furthermore provided suitable endowments of real estate and royal revenue for all churches, both those that the Church actually possessed and those that were to be restored (Art. 8).[140] Here again the Church maintained its rights in practice without making a definite statement of them.

There was no doubt, however, in the minds of churchmen what these rights were. The Council of Lyons (1850) stated as a fundamental principle that the Church, because it is a visible, perfect society, divinely established by Christ, is consequently of its very nature capable of ownership and of all the acts consequent upon ownership.[141] The provisions of the concordats were recognized as an acknowledgment of this inviolate right. The bishops held that the pension the government was to pay to the clergy took the place of the property possessed by the Church before the secularization; and pastors were ordered to administer the church property according to Church law and in such a manner as to safeguard the rights of the Church.[142]

After the law on the separation of the Church and the State was passed in 1905, there arose a need of a more explicit statement of church doctrine. The law was based on the principle that the

[139] Nussi, *Conventiones,* pp. 20–35.

[140] Nussi, *Conventiones,* p. 154.

[141] "Sicut nulla societas ex hominibus conflata potest subsistere nisi bona habeat, quibus valeat expensis necessariis providere, ita Ecclesia, quae est societas perfecta visibilis, propriae temporali existentiae consulens, et pauperibus quos semper secum habebit subveniens, ex Christi voluntate, non autem Principum concessione, ab initio fuit dominii capax, omnesque dominii actus semper exercuit. Quod expressis verbis et plurimae Sanctorum Pontificum Constitutiones et innumera sanxerunt Concilia, declarando res Ecclesiae esse Dei, utpote propter eius honorem Ecclesiae donatas, nec posse, sine sacrilegio invadi, rapi, aut ad saeculares usus converti—C. 23—*Coll. Lac.,* IV, 481.

[142] Provincial Council of Bourges (1850), Tit. VI, Decr. *De Oblationibus fidelium et Casuali—Coll. Lac.* IV, 1131; Provincial Council of Bordeaux (1850), Tit. 2, cap. I, n. 5—*Coll. Lac.* IV, 559.

State should no longer recognize the Catholic Church as a legal personality, but should recognize only individual, separate, lay associations for worship (*associations cultuelles*) that is to say, associations of laymen founded in each parish for the purpose of worship. The law made the formation of such associations obligatory. They were to take over all the property of the Church and to have complete charge of its administration. In case of the nonformation of these associations the property was to be forever lost to the Church and was to be turned over by decree to the charitable establishments of the various communes. As a result of the new law and the formation of the *associations cultuelles* the Church in France was stripped of most of its possessions and was barely tolerated in its religious edifices. Neither parish nor diocese could own land or fund, however small. The State insisted that only the *associations cultuelles* were to be clothed with the right of ownership for purposes of worship.

What was the reaction of the Church to this complete denial of its juridical personality and legal rights? It protested the new law, condemned and rejected it and reasserted its own right to have temporal goods. On February 21, 1906, Pope Pius X condemned the French laws of separation as a violation of Church rights and a diminution of her liberty. To strip the Church of the possession of the property legitimately acquired by it was against all justice, and contrary, in addition, to the express promises made by the French government. Consequently the Pope considered it his duty to condemn the law as favoring schism and opposed to international law.[143]

In two encyclical letters the Pope made it clear that he was protesting not only the seizure of church property, but especially the denial of the rights of the Church. He protested because the French government refused to acknowledge the juridical personality of the Church; because it would recognize only its own creatures, the *associations cultuelles,* as having the right to possess; and because it ordained that if the Church did not provide for the formation of such associations within a specified period of time, the government would seize its property and distribute it to civilly acknowledged juridical bodies.[144]

[143] Pius X, allocut., *"Gravissimum,"* 21 febr. 1906—*Fontes,* n. 672.

[144] Ep. encycl., *"Vehementer Nos,"* 11 febr. 1906—*Fontes,* n. 671; Litt. encycl., *"Une fois encore,"* 6 ian. 1907—*Fontes,* n. 677.

The Pope spoke because, in practice, the refusal to acknowledge the inherent right of the Church to possess and acquire property amounted to the spoliation of the Church. If the Church formed *associations cultuelles* its property passed from it to lay ownership and control; if it refused to form the associations it lost its property anyway. But it could not form those associations. They were contrary to its nature and its divine constitution. The Pope protested that in committing to these associations the possession and the administration of church property the civil government acted contrary to the inherent rights of the Church—rights that spring from its divine institution and are essential to it.[145]

His other encyclical letter on this question, "Vehementer Nos," of February 11, 1906, asserted that the Church had an inalienable right to the property that had been taken from her—a right that was based on the promises made by the French government in the concordat with the Holy See, on the clear legal titles which she had to all the property acquired by her, and on her own inherent right, the violation of which was a grave injustice.[146] In this way did the Roman Pontiff seek to maintain the inherent rights of the Church regarding the possession and the acquisition of property and to prevent their violation by the secular power. Even though all ecclesiastical buildings were confiscated the Church in France managed to benefit somewhat by its adversity; for although the government in depriving it of its possessions had impeded its work and restrained its influence, the civil authorities could no longer pretend to have the right to dictate to the Pope and to the bishops the selection of bishops and pastors.[147]

Spain.—Until the period of French control was ended in 1814 the policy followed in Spain in regard to church property was the same as that in France. Churches, monasteries, convents, and all lands belonging to the Church were secularized by the civil authorities. Upon the accession of Ferdinand II in 1814 the confiscated property was restored. Yet six years later elements hostile to the Catholic Church forced the suppression of the monasteries and the confiscation of church holdings. The theory that was accepted at

[145] Litt. encycl., *"Une fois encore,"* nn. 12, 13—*Fontes,* n. 677.

[146] N. 10—*Fontes,* n. 671.

[147] *Cf.* Poulet, *A History of the Catholic Church* (2 vols., St. Louis: B. Herder Book Co., 1934–1935), II, 467–468.

this time by the Spanish Cortes was that ownership of property by the Church (*i. e.*, by moral persons) was not real ownership, since the moral person was a mere creature of the civil law.[148] Consequently, the fate of ecclesiastical goods alternated between church ownership and confiscation until the concordat of 1851 was signed. Meanwhile the Popes, whenever opportunity offered, proclaimed the rights of the Church and protested the secularization of its property. In describing the secularization Pope Gregory XVI (1831–1846) adverted to the fact that it violated the rights of the Church.[149] A few years later he complained again that church property had been treated just as if it belonged to the secular authority and the Church did not have the native right to acquire temporal goods.[150] Finally, when the concordat was drawn up, it was stated explicitly that the Church had the right to acquire and to possess property. Article 41 definitely established the right of the Church to acquire temporal goods;[151] while article 40 provided for the independent administration of church property by the clergy. The words of the concordat, as Pope Pius IX later said, were a confirmation of the Church's inherent right to have temporal goods.[152]

In the September consistory of 1851, Pope Pius IX, after asserting the right that the Church has to acquire temporal goods, showed how that right was acknowledged in the concordat.[153]

[148] Liberatore, *L'Eglise et L'Etat,* liv. III, ch. I, p. 238.

[149] Allocut., *"Sextus iam,"* 1 febr. 1836—*Acta Gregorii XVI* (4 vols., Roma, 1901-1904), III, 93-94.

[150] Allocut., *"Afflictas,"* 1 mart. 1841, n. 6—*Fontes,* n. 496.

[151] "Ecclesia insuper ius habebit novas legitimo quovis titulo acquirendi possessiones; eiusque proprietas in omnibus quae nunc possidet, vel in posterum acquiret, inviolabilis erit."—*Raccolta,* p. 794.

[152] Allocut., *"Quibus luctuosissimis,"* 5 sept. 1851—*Fontes,* n. 512.

[153] "Omni enim studio et contentione vindicandum ac tuendum curabimus ius, quo Ecclesia pollet, acquirendi scilicet, et possidendi quaecumque bona stabilia et frugifera, veluti innumera prope Conciliorum acta et Sanctorum Patrum sententiae et exempla, Praedecessorum Nostrorum Constitutiones apertissime loquuntur, sapientissime docent et demonstrant . . . Iam porro in Conventione constabilitum firmatumque conspicietis Ecclesiae ius novas acquirendi possessiones ac simul sancitum ut proprietas bonorum omnium quae vel in praesentia possidet, vel in posterum acquiret integra et inviolabilis omnino habeat atque persistat."—Allocut., *"Quibus luctuosissimis,"*—*Fontes,* n. 512.

This concordat stood as a fixed statement of Church rights throughout the troublesome years that followed its ratification. When in 1854 a hostile Cortes nullified articles 1 and 2 of the concordat and ordered the confiscation and sale of church property, the Pope withdrew the Papal Nuncio from Madrid in protest. In the consistory of July, 1855, he declared the "usurpation of the patrimony of the Church contrary to all divine and human law," and condemned the decrees of the Cortes.[154] Because of the strained relations between Spain and the Holy See that followed the passage of these decrees, a new concordat was deemed advisable. In 1859 it was completed and ratified as a "supplementary pact to the concordat of 1851," which together with the older concordat was to be regarded as part of the law of Spain.[155] The new concordat was very explicit in its recognition of the Church's right to acquire temporal goods without limitation or reservation.[156]

In spite of this recognition of Church rights, which was also the law of the State, secularization laws continued to be decreed, and the Pope was forced to assert the rights of the Church once more. In an encyclical, *"Incredibile,"* issued in 1863, Pius IX, as he had done so often before, condemned those laws which violated Church rights by usurping and secularizing Church property. Once again he vindicated "the legitimate right of the Church to acquire and to possess." [157]

The concordat of 1851 continued to be the basic law regulating the relations between the Church and the State. When specific problems arose, however, they were settled by separate agreements, as, for example, the agreement of 1904, which recognized the juridical personality of religious communities.[158]

The extent of recognition granted to the Church's right to acquire has been uncertain since the proclamation of the Spanish republic in 1931. It may be expected, however, that a result of negotiations now being carried on between the Holy See and the Spanish government will be a new and definite restatement of the native right of the Church to acquire temporal goods.

[154] Allocut., *"Nemo Vestrum,"* 26 iul. 1855—*Pii IX Pontificis Maximi Acta* (7 vols., Romae, n.d.), II, 441–446.

[155] Art. 21—Nussi, *Conventiones,* 345.

[156] Art. 3, 4—Nussi, *Conventiones,* 341.

[157] *Fontes,* n. 537.

[158] Art. 1—*Raccolta,* p. 1902.

Portugal.—In the eighteenth century Portugal witnessed the appropriation by the State of the property of the Jesuits, a result of Pombal's (1699–1782) hatred of the society and thoroughly Gallican attitude toward the Church. Although there is no record of a concordat between the Holy See and Portugal, the differences between the two sovereignties were settled gradually by Popes Clement XIII (1758–1769) and Clement XIV (1769–1774).

The most serious denial of Church rights occurred in 1911, when the complete separation of Church and State was decreed. Portugal, it was declared, was no longer to be bound to the observance of the Catholic religion; churches, chapels, lands, hitherto applied to the public worship of the Catholic religion, were declared to be the property of the State, unless *bona fide* ownership by some private individual or legally recognized corporation could be proved. The juridical personality of the Church or of moral persons within the Church was no longer recognized. Boards of laymen (after the manner of the French *associations cultuelles*) were to assume the administration of the temporalities necessary for worship; but this arrangement was not stable, as it was revocable at the pleasure of the government. The new laws not only violated the right to possess, they prevented the Church from acquiring any property in the future. They practically denied the juridical personality of the Catholic Church. Pope Pius X described the state of affairs as follows: ". . . huius praescripto legis, non solum quascumque res Ecclesia mobiles, immobiles obtinet, ex earum possessione quamvis optimo iure parta, detruditur; verum etiam quaevis ei potestas adimitur quidquam sibi in posterum acquirendi." The Pope protested this violation of the right to acquire property, and, motivated by a desire to preserve the rights of the Church, condemned the laws of separation.[159]

Germany and Austria.—In Germany and Austria the nineteenth century witnessed the growth of the secularization of church property that had been begun toward the end of the eighteenth century. The Napoleonic government's favorite way of compensating the smaller German states for territory that had been taken from them was to secularize church property. The compensation thus granted the temporal princes was at the expense of the Church.

[159] Litt. encycl., *"Iamdudum,"* 24 maii 1911, nn. 3, 7—*Fontes*, n. 692.

In 1802, at a meeting in Regensburg to discuss the secularization of church property, Napoleon said that "ecclesiastical suzerainties were not in keeping with the spirit of the Gospel," and proceeded by means of secret treaties to restore the Church to what he might have called "its evangelical integrity." He thus accomplished the seizure of a great part of church property in what was modern Germany before 1937. Lands, buildings, episcopal palaces, abbeys, churches, objects of art, libraries, etc., were seized and sold. It must not be forgotten that no compensation was made for these seizures. The secularization was "justified" by theories that were directly opposed to the divine institution and to the inherent rights of the Church—theories which refused to recognize the Church as having any juridical personality except that which it pleased the State to grant or accord to it.

As a consequence not only of secularization, but especially of the erroneous teachings that prompted it, the Roman Pontiffs were careful, whenever they were given the opportunity to restore friendly relations with the civil governments, to state explicitly the inherent rights of the Church—rights that belonged to the Church by nature, rights that were not granted to it by any civil power. Thus the concordat between Pius VII and Maximillian Joseph of Bavaria (1817) insisted that the Church have the right to acquire possessions, and provided specifically for the conservation of ecclesiastical properties.[160]

Article 12 of the concordat with Frederick of Baden (1859) recognized the right of the Church to possess, to acquire, and to administer its own property.[161] Unfortunately, however, the concordat was shortlived. The liberal party, motivated by an anti-Catholic spirit, nullified it and secularized many ecclesiastical institutions. Catholic churches were even given by the government to schismatic and heretical sects.

The concordat with Austria in 1855 explicitly safeguarded ecclesiastical rights to the acquisition, ownership, and administration of temporal goods. Article 29 made the following declaration: "Ecclesia iure suo pollebit, novas iusto quovis titulo libere acquirendi possessiones eiusque proprietas in omnibus, quae nunc possidet, vel imposterum acquiret, inviolabilis solemniter erit . . ."

[160] *Raccolta,* p. 594.

[161] *Ibid.,* p. 888.

Article 30 provided: "Bonorum ecclesiasticorum administratio apud eos erit ad quos secundum canones spectat." [162]

The doctrine on which the provisions of these concordats were founded was carefully explained by the bishops in diocesan and provincial councils, and in letters addressed to the civil authorities regarding the observance of the concordat. In 1856, for instance, the Austrian bishops in a letter to the Minister of Worship and Education showed that the Church as a human society had need of temporal goods to attain its end, and therefore had the right to acquire and possess them; it had a right to enjoy full property rights and to administer its possessions according to its own laws. The concordat, they said, had recognized and sanctioned these fundamental principles for which the Austrian bishops had so long fought.[163] A similar stand had been taken by the bishops when, in 1848, they had addressed the Reichstag.[164]

The provincial synods of Germany, Holland and Austria during the nineteenth century are notable for their exposition of the Catholic doctrine on the rights of the Church. They not only assert the legal capacity of the Church to acquire and own property, but they give the rational basis for ecclesiastical ownership. Thus the provincial council of Utrecht (1865):

> Ecclesia a Christo Domino fundata et instituta tamquam societas perfecta, quum ad salutis ministerium in terris exercendum terrenis etiam egeat praesidiis, temporalia bona, iure sibi proprio, acquirit, ac possidet. Deo dedicata, ecclesiastica bona splendori cultus, pietatis operibus, ministrorum sustentationi impenduntur, et sacra eo ipso sunt, quod ad hos religiosos usus destinantur. Nefas est, nisi legitima accedente auctoritate legitimisque suffragantibus causis, ab usu ad quem adhibenda sunt illa distrahere.[165]

The same Council refuted those who would restrict the Church's activity to praying and preaching, and proclaimed that since the Church was established in this world, and consists of men who live in this world, it necessarily possesses the right to acquire

[162] Nussi, *Conventiones,* p. 316.

[163] *Coll. Lac.,* V, 1275.

[164] Adresse des Episcopats der Salzburger Kirchenprovinz an den Reichstag zu Wien, 14 September, 1848—*Coll. Lac.,* V, 1322.

[165] Tit. X, cap. 1—*Coll. Lac.,* V, 922.

temporal goods; for, such goods are the means to be used by it to attain its end.[166]

Other councils asserted the Church's right freely to acquire property (so that its ownership is inviolate) and to obtain pious endowments. The bishops who met at Freising in 1850 set forth the fundamental principles on which the Church's property rights are based, and insisted that Article 8 of the Bavarian concordat be observed strictly by the government.[167] The Salzburg synod of 1848 reaffirmed the legitimate capacity of the Church to own property, and defended the Church against the claims of the civil power.[168] The Bishops defended the Catholic teaching that the universal Church is the subject of property rights and of ownership, contrary to the Protestant doctrine which says that the subject of these rights is the universal parish. They claimed also the right of the Church freely to administer its property and to be protected by the civil power in the exercise of these rights.[169] The Council of Cologne (1848) decreed that the Church must be allowed freedom to acquire property.[170] The Council of Vienna (1849) defended the rights of ownership that belonged to the Church.[171]

Likewise other German councils of the same period vindicated the right of the Church not only to acquire and to possess property, but to be free from interference from the civil power in the exercise of that right.[172]

In the following century the right that had been so vigorously upheld by these councils was solemnly recognized by the civil powers. In 1925 Bavaria recognized the right of the Church to acquire and possess property.[173] In 1929 Prussia guaranteed the

[166] Tit. I, cap. 9—*Coll. Lac.*, V, 766.

[167] Conventus Episcoporum Bavariae Frisingensis—*Coll. Lac.*, V, 1185–1186.

[168] *Coll. Lac.*, V, 1322.

[169] Council of Würzburg (1848)—*Coll. Lac.*, V, 1137.

[170] *Coll. Lac.*, V, 944.

[171] *Coll. Lac.*, V, 1354.

[172] Cologne (1849)—*Coll. Lac.*, V, 1151–1152; Freising (1850)—*ibid.*, 1185–1186; Freiburg (1851)—*ibid.*, 1216; Vienna (1858)—*ibid.*, 1255, 1275; Goerz (1848)—*ibid.*, 1330.

[173] Concordat of 1925, Art. 10, § 4—*AAS*, XVII (1925), 50.

property rights of ecclesiastical goods.[174] Baden did the same in 1932,[175] and in 1933 in the concordat between the Holy See and the German Reich the juridical personality and the property rights of ecclesiastical institutions were acknowledged and guaranteed.[176] Finally, the right of the Church to acquire and possess property was recognized anew in Austria also.[177]

Italy.—In 1764 the duke of Parma forbade the transfer of the use or ownership of property to ecclesiastical hands. The only property that could be given to churchmen or church corporations was a sum of money equivalent to one-twentieth of the total estate of the donor. But this grant was further restricted by the provision that the sum so given was not to exceed 300 scudi. In 1767 another edict renewed the edict of 1764 regarding the acquisition of property by the Church; but it allowed churchmen to be the beneficiaries of their relatives, provided that they did not transfer their inheritance to the Church. A second edict of the same year presumed to set up a lay superintendent to oversee the administration of church property, the payment of church revenues, etc. These laws considerably limited the power of the Church to acquire possessions. They allowed only 300 scudi to be acquired from any individual. While this provision can be said implicitly to recognize the right of the Church to acquire, yet its tone suggests the theory that this right is ultimately subject to the control of the political power. Certainly the limitation of the amount of property that could be acquired by the Church constituted a violation of its inherent right to acquire. This was the view of the then reigning Pope, Clement XIII, who said that the edicts were issued *contra Ecclesiae iura et libertatem.* He condemned them because they prejudiced the liberty, immunity, and rights of the Church.[178]

On the other hand, the government of Naples in the concordat of 1818 solemnly recognized the fundamental right of the Church to acquire temporal possessions. Article 15 stated: "Ecclesia ius

[174] Concordat, Art. 5—Giannini, *I Concordati Postbellici* (2 vols., Milano: "Vita e Pensiero" 1929-1936), II, 160.

[175] Concordat, Art. 5—Giannini, *op. cit.*, II, 242.

[176] Art. 13, 17—Giannini, *op. cit.*, II, 426-427.

[177] Concordat, Art. 13, § 1—*AAS*, XXVI (1934), 264.

[178] Constit., *"Alias ad Apostolatus,"* 30 ian. 1768—*Fontes,* n. 464.

habebit novas acquirendi possessiones, et quidquid de novo acquisierit faciet suum et censebitur eodem iure ac veteres fundationes ecclesiasticae." In article 26 the inviolability of this right was recognized: "Ecclesiae proprietas in suis possessionibus, et acquisitionibus sacra et inviolabilis erit." [179]

In 1841 Modena recognized the right of the Church to acquire property by repealing the mortmain tax and the prohibition against transfers or bequests of property to ecclesiastical corporations.[180]

Despite such recognition, which was the result of the Popes' defense of Church rights, the growing Nationalism, indoctrinated as it was with Liberalism, threatened the existence of ecclesiastical property throughout Italy. Pope Pius IX (1846–1878) recognized the danger and warned against it. As far as property was concerned he warned that the liberalist aim was to despoil the "Catholic Church of its just possessions." [181]

After the Nationalists had seized a part of the Papal States (1861) the Pope was urged to seek a reconciliation with them. But he refused because the seizure was an unjust act. The demand for a reconciliation he unmasked as an attempt to force the Holy See to condone the seizures and to acknowledge the usurpers as legitimate owners of the Papal provinces. Instead, he condemned the usurpation as violence and injustice, and demanded the restitution of the seized provinces.[182] The Papal States, he declared the next year, were providentially given to the Holy See, and helped to maintain that liberty of action which was necessary for the fulfillment of the Church's mission on earth.[183] By usurping the territory that belonged to the Church the Nationalists, in the words of the Sovereign Pontiff, "sacrilego auso omnia ipsius Ecclesiae iura et leges quotidie magis proculcaverunt." They denied the personality of the Church, and taught that it is not a

[179] Nussi, *Conventiones,* 183–186; article 26 appears as article 27 in Mercati's *Raccolta,* p. 634.

[180] Decreto del Duca Francesco—*Raccolta,* p. 742.

[181] Allocut., *"Iamdudum cernimus,"* 18 mart. 1861—*Fontes,* n. 530.

[182] *Fontes,* n. 530.

[183] Allocut., *"Maxima quidem,"* 9 iun. 1862, n. 6—*Fontes,* n. 534. Although the temporal dominion of the Popes in the Papal States may be called providential, it cannot be said to be of divine right. Else the Church would have lacked an essential feature for several centuries.—Augustine, *Commentary,* VI, 553.

perfect and free society with its own immutable rights, but that it belongs to the civil power to define what are the rights of the Church and the limits within which it may exercise them.[184]

The Nationalists, in accordance with their political theories, decreed the seized provinces to be the property of the State and prepared to sell not only the lands but even the Church edifices and estates to private individuals. Pius IX lashed out against this in the consistory of September 20, 1867.[185] As the law did not apply to private property, but to all ecclesiastically owned properties, both in the newly acquired Papal provinces and in the Kingdom of Piedmont, it violated an inherent right which flowed from the divine constitution of the Church; for it subordinated the right to acquire property to the recognition of a political power.[186]

The rights of the Church were not recognized until the Lateran Treaty and the Concordat with Italy were signed in 1929. By the former treaty Vatican City State was erected, and the sovereignty of the Holy See was recognized. Moreover, Italy recognized the full property rights of the Holy See to the territory of Vatican City as well as to certain other parcels of real estate within the Kingdom of Italy.[187] The concordat acknowledged the juridical status of moral persons within the Church and recognized their right to acquire and to possess property. Article 30 reads as follows: "Lo Stato italiano riconosce agli istituti ecclesiastici ed alle associazioni religiose la capacita di acquistare beni, salve le disposizioni delle leggi civili concernenti gli acquisti dei corpi morali." [188]

H. The Right to Acquire in Some Recent Concordats

As a consequence of the doctrine that ecclesiastical moral persons derive their juridical personality from the State, and of the extensive violations of the rights of the Church which followed the almost general acceptance of that doctrine by civil lawyers and

184 *Fontes,* n. 534.

185 *Cf.* allocut., *"Universus catholicus orbis,"* 20 sept. 1867—*Fontes,* n. 547.

186 "Omnes profecto vident quam iniusta et quam immanis sit haec lex qua . . . inviolabile possidendi ius, quo Ecclesia ex divina sua institutione pollet, oppugnatur."—*Fontes,* n. 547.

187 *AAS,* XXI (1929), 209–211.

188 *AAS,* XXI (1929), 288; Giannini, *I Concordati Postbellici,* II, 107.

governments, papal pronouncements became increasingly insistent upon the native right of the Church to acquire temporal goods. Gregory XVI in his allocution of March 1, 1841, *"Afflictas,"* complained that church property had been usurped by civil rulers "just as if it had belonged to the political power, and the Church did not have the native right to acquire and possess temporal goods." [189] Pius IX not only referred to the right of the Church to acquire temporal goods as a "legitimate right," [190] but also stressed the fact that it was a native right and had been acknowledged as such in the concordat with Spain in 1851.[191] Later in his *"Syllabus errorum"* he condemned the proposition: "The Church does not have a native and legitimate right to acquire and possess." [192] In the encyclical *"Quanta cura"* (Dec. 8, 1864) the same Pontiff explained that the Church possesses the right to acquire because its Founder, when He established it, endowed it with the right. As a result of this divine endowment it depends in no way upon the civil authority for the capacity to acquire temporal goods, and whenever it vindicates its right it is by no means usurping or encroaching upon the rights of civil powers. It is therefore erroneous, the Pontiff continued, to assert that "it is in conformity with the principles of theology and law to vindicate and claim for the civil government the ownership of property held by churches, religious communities, and other pious places." [193]

The Vatican Council had prepared a very strong statement of the Church's right to own property and of its independence of the State in this matter: "We teach that the Church, as a visible society established by God among men, has the right to acquire and to possess temporal goods, and cannot be deprived of that right by any secular power. Moreover, . . . we declare that the laws according to which the political state, as if by supreme inherent right, usurps ecclesiastical property are unjust spoliations." [194] Moreover, the Council was prepared to condemn the false teaching which, denying that the Church is a perfect society,

[189] *Fontes,* n. 496, § 6.

[190] Encycl., *"Incredibili,"* 17 sept. 1863—*Pii IX P. M. Acta,* III, 622–628.

[191] Allocut., *"Nemo Vestrum,"* 26 iul. 1855—*Pii IX P. M. Acta,* II, 441–446; allocut., *"Numquam fore,"* 15 dec. 1856—*Op. cit.,* II, 547.

[192] Prop. 26—*Denz.* n. 1726; *Fontes,* n. 543.

[193] *Fontes,* n. 542; *Denz.* n. 1697.

[194] *Coll. Lac.,* VII, 576.

contended that the Church, because it exists within the State, is thereby subject to the State.[195] Due to the suspension of the Vatican Council this *schema* never became law. Yet it has value as showing the teaching of the bishops of the universal Church in council assembled on the question of Church property rights.

The insistence upon the native right of the Church to acquire property was reflected in local councils, which incorporated into their legislation an explanation and defense of the right. Thus the Provincial Council of Utrecht (1865) asserted that the right to acquire temporal goods was a *ius proprium* and flowed from the very nature of the Church as a society.[196] The necessity for temporal goods as means to the end established by Christ was declared by the Council of Salzburg (1848) to give the Church a legitimate right to acquire.[197] The right to acquire was further defended by the councils of Freising (1850) and Vienna (1856).[198] In the United States the II Plenary Council of Baltimore (1866) upheld the right of the Church to acquire temporal goods.[199] The bishops of the I Plenary Council of Baltimore (1852) had declared that all things given to the Church for the purposes of divine worship or for the maintenance of the clergy and church institutions were "res sacrae" and became the *property* of the Church.[200] The III Plenary Council of Baltimore (1884) declared: "We must hold holily and inviolably that the complete right of *ownership* and *dominion* over ecclesiastical goods resides in the Church." [201] The right of the Church to possess (which implies the right to acquire) temporal goods was upheld by councils in Canada, England, and Ireland.[202]

The concordats of the past hundred years show the results of this continual insistence by ecclesiastical authority upon the native

[195] Si quis dixerit Ecclesiam non esse societatem perfectam sed collegium; aut ita in civili societati seu in statu esse, ut seculari dominationi subiciatur: anathema sit.—canon X. *Coll. Lac.*, VII, 577.

[196] Tit. I, cap. 9: tit. X, cap. 1—*Coll. Lac.*, V, 766, 922.

[197] *Coll. Lac.*, V, 1322.

[198] *Coll. Lac.*, V, 1185–1186; V, 1275.

[199] Tit. IV, nn. 199–200—*Coll. Lac.*, III, 454.

[200] *Coll. Lac.*, III. 1146.

[201] Tit. IX, n. 264.

[202] II Provincial Council of Quebec (1854)— *Coll. Lac.*, III, 657; Provincial Synod of Westminster (1855)—*ibid.*, 980; Plenary Council of Ireland—*ibid.*, 793.

right of the Church to acquire. Many concordats expressly recognize this native right as such. The concordat with Spain in 1851 is a notable example.[203] The Austrian concordat of 1855 recognized the right of the Church to acquire as the Church's own proper right (ius suum).[204] Likewise the concordats with Ecuador (1862, 1881),[205] Serbia (1914),[206] Poland (1925),[207] Lithuania (1927) [208] and Italy (1929) [209] acknowledge that the right of the Church to acquire temporal goods is a right which belongs to the Church. The concordats with the Latin American countries generally recognize the right of the Church to acquire "quovis iusto titulo"—which is an implicit acknowledgment that the right is a native right of the Church and not a right that has been acquired from the civil government.[210]

A new trend would appear to be evidenced by some recent concordats in which the civil government agrees that the ownership and other property rights of the Church will be "guaranteed according to the civil law of the State." There is no explicit mention of the native right of the Church, but the right to acquire is recognized within the limits allowed by the civil law.[211] Can it be argued, from this silence about the native right, that the Church in these cases has renounced its native right and that in these countries the right of the Church to acquire is derived from the civil law? The wording of the concordats might seem to indicate that the right of the Church to acquire is actually derived from the State, since only those possessions of the Church are guaranteed and protected which have been or will be acquired in accordance with the law of the country.

The traditional stand of the Church, as evidenced by history, is

[203] *Cf. supra* p. 85.

[204] *Raccolta,* p. 827.

[205] *Raccolta,* pp. 992, 1011.

[206] *Raccolta,* p. 1103.

[207] *AAS,* XVII (1925), 279.

[208] *AAS,* XIX (1927), 430.

[209] *AAS,* XXI (1929), 288.

[210] Costa Rica (1852)—*Raccolta,* p. 806; Guatemala (1852)—*ibid.,* p. 818; Honduras (1861)—*ibid.,* p. 943; Nicaragua (1861)—*ibid.,* p. 955; San Salvador (1862)—*ibid.,* p. 967; Venezuela (1862)—*ibid.,* p. 977.

[211] *E. g.,* concordats with Austria (1934)—*AAS,* XXVI (1934), 264; Prussia (1929)—*AAS,* XXI (1929), 526; Germany (1933)—*AAS,* XXV (1933), 399.

opposed to such a conclusion, however. The Church has consistently upheld its right to acquire, and has ever defended its independence from the civil power. The purpose of concordats, moreover, is to assure that independence. Were the Church to submit to the pretensions of the State as to the right to acquire property its independence would be doomed.

If such a conclusion were allowed the concordats would openly conflict with the canon law of the Church. Since the promulgation of the Code it has been the desire of the Holy See that all new particular legislation should accord with the canons as much as possible. In view of this it is inconceivable that the Holy See would renounce or even compromise a right that is of so fundamental importance.

What then does the restrictive phrasing of these recent concordats signify? It means that in the concordats the Holy See, while maintaining the right of the Church to acquire, agrees to comply with the formalities of the civil law in order to provide greater security for her possessions. If ecclesiastical goods have been acquired according to the civil law the Church is enabled to defend them even in the civil courts.

This explanation accords with the explanation of the concordat with Ecuador given by Pius X to the bishops of that country in 1905. The concordat with Ecuador had recognized the right of the Church to acquire property by every just title consonant with the laws of the Republic. When the property of the Church was appropriated in violation of the provisions of the concordat, the Pope reminded the people of Ecuador that the Church did not thereby lose its property; that the Church could still legitimately acquire temporal goods; and that the faithful would be obliged to come to the aid of the Church if it were reduced to need as a result of the depredations of the civil power.[212]

Commentators even before the Code held that if the Church should agree to comply with the civil law, it would do so not in sign of recognition that its right to acquire was derived from the civil law, but merely to give its property the protection of the civil law.[213] The guarantees provided for in the recent concordats do

[212] Ep., *"Acre nefariumque,"* 10 maii 1905—*Fontes,* n. 668.

[213] *E. g.,* Wernz, *Ius Decretalium,* III, n. 135; Cavagnis, *Institutiones Iuris Publici Ecclesiastici,* III, n. 394.

not, therefore, represent a departure from the traditional defense of the right to acquire, but are to be interpreted as guarantees of protection and security to be afforded by the State to church property.

In the concordats, therefore, the policy of the Church has ever been to state its rights prudently, to have the civil power recognize them, and to safeguard them with the protection of the civil law. The claim of the Church has always been the same: It possesses the native right, freely and independently of the civil power, to acquire temporal goods.

CONCLUSIONS

1. Gospel texts such as Matt., x, 10; Luke, x, 7; John, xii, 6; xiii, 29; and others of like content prove only the right of the minister of the Gospel to support and maintenance.

2. The divine right of the Church to acquire property is proved solely and sufficiently from the fact of its establishment by Christ as a perfect society.

3. No argument based entirely upon natural law and reason can adequately establish the right of the *supernatural* society that is the Church; yet, if the Church be regarded as a human society, according to natural law and reason it has at least as much right to acquire property as any human society.

4. The provisions of some recent concordats, by which the Church agrees to limit its acquisition of property to the modes recognized in the civil law, are not contrary to its native right to acquire, and cannot be alleged as indications that the right of the Church in those countries is derived from the civil law of the land.

BIBLIOGRAPHY

Sources

Acta Apostolicae Sedis, Commentarium Officiale, Romae, 1909—

Acta et Decreta Concilii Plenarii Baltimorensis Tertii (1884), Baltimorae, 1886.

Acta et Decreta Sacrorum Conciliorum Recentiorum, Collectio Lacensis, 7 vols., Friburgi Brisgoviae, 1870–1890.

Acta Gregorii Papae XVI, 4 vols., Romae, 1901–1904.

Acta Sanctae Sedis, 41 vols., Romae, 1865–1908.

Anselmi Lucensis, *Collectio Canonum* (Ed. Fredericus Thaner), 2 vols., Oeniponte, 1906, 1915.

Bullarium Romanum, Editio Taurinensis, 25 vols., Augustae Taurinorum, 1857–1872.

Clementis VIII, *Decretales* (edidit Franciscus Sentis), Friburgi Brisgoviae, 1870.

Codex Iuris Canonici Pii X Pontificis Maximi iussu digestus Benedicti Papae XV auctoritate promulgatus, Romae: Typis Polyglottis Vaticanis, 1934.

Codicis Iuris Canonici Fontes cura Emi Petri Card. Gasparri editi, 9 vols., Romae: Typis Polyglottis Vaticanis, 1923–1939. (Vol. VII–IX ed. cura et studio Emi Iustiniani Card. Serédi.)

Collectanea S. Congregationis de Propaganda Fide, 2 vols., Romae 1907.

Concilium Tridentinum, Diariorum, Actorum, Epistularum Nova Collectio, edidit Societas Goerresiana, 13 tomes, Friburgi Brisgoviae, 1901–1938.

Corpus Iuris Civilis, 3 vols., Berolini, 1928–1929.
Institutiones, quas recognovit P. Krueger;
Digesta, quae recognovit et retractavit P. Krueger;
Codex Iustinianus, quem recognovit et retractavit P. Krueger;
Novellae, quas recognovit R. Schoell et absolvit G. Kroll.

Denzinger—Bannwart—Umberg, *Enchiridion Symbolorum et Definitionum,* editio 21–23, Friburgi Brisgoviae: Herder & Co., 1937.

Digard—Faucon—Thomas, *Les Registres de Boniface VIII,* 4 vols., Bordeaux, n.d.

Evans, William David, *A Collection of Statutes,* 8 vols., London, 1817.

Giannini, Amedeo, *I Concordati Postbellici,* 2 vols., Milano: "Vita e Pensiero," 1929, 1936.

Haddan, A. W.—Stubbs, W., *Councils and Ecclesiastical Documents relating to Great Britain and Ireland,* 3 vols., Oxford, 1869–1873.

Harduin, Joannes, *Acta Conciliorum et Epistolae Decretales,* 12 vols., Parisiis, 1715.

Krueger, P., *Codex Theodosianus,* Berolini: apud Weidmannos, 1923–1926.

SS. D. N. Leonis XIII Acta, 6 vols., Brugis et Insulis, 1887–1900.

Mansi, Joannes, *Sacrorum Conciliorum nova et amplissima collectio,* 53 vols., Parisiis, 1901–1927.

Mercati, Angelo, *Raccolta di Concordati,* Roma: Tipografia Poliglotta Vaticana, 1919.

Nussi, Vincentius, *Conventiones de Rebus Ecclesiasticis,* Mainz, 1870.

Pii IX Pontificis Maximi Acta, 7 vols., Romae, n.d.

Richter, A. L.—Friedberg, A., *Corpus Iuris Canonici,* 2 vols., Lipsiae, 1879, 1881.

Theiner, Augustinus, *Acta Authentica SS. Oecumenici Concilii Tridentini,* 2 vols., Zagabriae, 1874.

Thiel, Andreas, *Epistolae Romanorum Pontificum Genuinae,* vol. 1, Brunsbergae, 1868.

Authors

Affre, *Traité de la Propriété des Biens Ecclésiastiques,* Paris, 1837.

Allen, Willoughby C., *A Critical and Exegetical Commentary on the Gospel According to S. Matthew,* New York, 1907.

Ales, Adhemer d', *Dictionnaire Apologetique de la Foi Catholique,* 4 vols., Paris: Gabriel Beauchesne & Cie., 1911–1922.

Andre, Michel, *Dictionnaire de Droit Canon,* 2 vols., Paris, 1844.

Audisio, Guillaume, *Droit Public de L'Église,* 3 vols., Louvain, 1864–1865.

[Bachofen,] Charles Augustine, *A Commentary on the New Code of Canon Law,* vol. 6 (*Administrative Law*), 2. ed., St. Louis: B. Herder Book Co., 1923.

Bachofen, Augustinus, *Summa Iuris Ecclesiastici Publici,* Romae, 1910.

Barbosa, Augustinus, *Ius Ecclesiasticum Universum,* 2 vols., Lugduni, 1650–1660.

Bargilliat, M., *Praelectiones Juris Canonici,* vol. 1, Parisiis: Baston, Berche et Pagis, 1923–1924.

Barile, Alexander, *De Patrimoniali Ecclesiae Regimine,* Romae: Athenaeum, 1925.

Baronius, Caesar, Card., *Annales Ecclesiastici,* 37 vols., Barri-Ducis, 1864–1883.

Bartlett, Chester Joseph, *The Tenure of Parochial Property in the United States,* The Catholic University of America, Canon Law Studies, n. 31, Washington, D. C.: The Catholic University of America, 1927.

Batiffol, Pierre, *Primitive Catholicism,* translated from the fifth French edition, New York, 1911.

Bellarmino, Roberto, Card., *Opera Omnia,* 8 vols., Neapoli, 1872.

Blat, Albertus, *Commentarium Textus Codicis Iuris Canonici,* 6 vols., Romae: Typographia Pontificia in Instituto Pii IX, 1921–1927.

Bonfante, Pietro, *Istituzioni di Diritto Romano,* Roma: Istituto di Diritto Romano, 1934.

Brown, Brendan Francis, *The Canonical Juristic Personality,* The Catholic University of America, Canon Law Studies, n. 39, Washington, D. C.: The Catholic University of America, 1927.

Campomanes, Pedro R., *Tratado de la regalia de amortizacion,* Madrid, 1821.
Cappello, Felix, *Summa Iuris Publici Ecclesiastici,* Romae: Apud Aedes Universitatis Gregorianae, 1928.
Carrière, Joseph, *De Iustitia et Iure,* 3 vols., Parisiis, 1839.
Catholic Encyclopedia, The, 16 vols., New York, 1907–1912.
Cavagnis, Felix, *Institutiones Iuris Publici Ecclesiastici,* 3 vols., Romae, 1906.
———, *Nozioni di Diritto Publico Naturale ed Ecclesiastico,* Roma, 1886.
Choupin, Lucien, *Valeur des Décisions Doctrinales et Disciplinaires du Saint-Siège,* Paris: Gabriel Beauchesne, 1928.
Contreras, C. Rafael, *La iglesia y sus bienes,* Mexico: Universidad Nacional de Mexico, 1933.
Cornely, Rudolphus, *Commentarius in S. Pauli Apostoli Epistolas,*
I *Epistola ad Romanos,* Parisiis, 1896;
II *Prior Epistola ad Corinthios,* Parisiis, 1890.
Coronata, Matthaeus Conte a, *Institutiones Iuris Canonici,* vol. II, 2. ed., Taurini: Marietti, 1939.
———, *Ius Publicum Ecclesiasticum,* Taurini: Marietti, 1924.
Coulondre, Gaston, *Des Acquisitions des Biens par les Etablissements de la Religion Chretienne,* Paris, 1886.
Coviello, Nicola—Del Giudice, Vincenzo, *Manuale di Diritto Ecclesiastico,* 2 vols., Romae: Athenaeum, 1922.
Daris, J., *La Liberté de la Religion Catholique,* Liége, 1865.
Dausch, Petrus, *Die Drei Aelteren Evangelien,* Bonn: Verlag von Peter Hanstein, 1923.
De Luise, Gaspar, *De Iure Publico seu Diplomatico Ecclesiae Catholicae,* Napoli, 1877.
Del Giudice, Vincenzo, *Istituzioni di Diritto Canonico,* vol. 1, Milano: Tenconi, 1929.
De Meester, A., *Juris Canonici et Juris Canonico-civilis Compendium,* 4 vols., Brugis: Desclée de Brouwer, 1921–1928.
Devoti, Joannes, *Institutiones Canonicae,* Ed. 4 Veneta, 4 vols., Venetiis, 1827.
Dieckmann, Hermannus, *De Ecclesia,* 2 vols., Friburgi Brisgoviae: Herder & Co., 1925.
Doheny, William J., *Church Property: Modes of Acquisition,* The Catholic University of America, Canon Law Studies, n. 41, Washington, D. C.: The Catholic University of America, 1927.
Duchesne, Louis, *Early History of the Christian Church,* New York, 1909.
———, *Le Liber Pontificalis,* 2 vols., Paris, 1886.
Eichmann, Eduard, *Quellensammlung zur kirchliche Rechtsgeschichte und zum Kirchenrecht, Kirche und Staat,* vol. I, 2 ed., Paderborn, 1925; vol. II, 1 ed., Paderborn, 1914.
———, *Lehrbuch des Kirchenrechts,* 2 ed., Paderborn: Ferdinand Schoeningh, 1926.
Enciclopedia Italiana, 35 vols., Roma: Istituto Giovani Treccani, 1929–1937.
Ferraris, F. Lucius, *Bibliotheca Canonica,* 9 vols., Romae, 1885–1899.
Ferreres, Joannes B., *Institutiones Canonicae,* vol. 2, Barcinone, 1920.

Friedberg, Emil, *Lehrbuch des katholischen und evangelischen Kirchenrechts,* Leipzig, 1903.

Grotius, Hugo, *De Imperio Summarum Potestatum circa Sacra,* Parisiis, 1647.

Hannan, Jerome Daniel, *The Canon Law of Wills,* The Catholic University of America, Canon Law Studies, n. 86, Washington, D. C.: The Catholic University of America, 1934.

Haring, Johann B., *Grundzuege des katholischen Kirchenrechts,* 2 vols., Graz: Ulrich Moser, 1924.

Hergenroether, Philipp, *Lehrbuch des katholischen Kirchenrechts,* Freiburg im Breisgau, 1888.

Hergenroether, P.—Hollweck, J., *Lehrbuch des katholischen Kirchenrechts,* 2 ed., Freiburg im Breisgau, 1905.

Hericourt, Louis de, *Les Loix Ecclésiastiques,* Paris, 1771.

Huebler, J., *Der Eigenthuemer des Kirchengutes,* Leipzig, 1868.

Hummelauer, Franciscus de, *Commentarius in Numeros,* Parisiis, 1899.

Knabenbauer, Joseph, *Commentarius in Quattuor S. Evangelia,*
I *Evangelium Secundum S. Matthaeum,* pars prior, Parisiis, 1892;
III *Evangelium Secundum Lucam,* Pariis, 1896.

———, *Commentarius in Actus Apostolorum,* Parisiis, 1899.

Lagrange, M. J., *Évangile selon Saint Matthieu,* Paris: Librairie Lecoffre, 1927.

———, *Évangile selon Saint Jean,* Paris: Librairie Lecoffre, 1927.

Liberatore, M., *Le Droit Public de L'Église* (translated into French by Aug. Onclair), Paris, 1888.

———, *L'Église et L'État* (French translation of second Italian edition), Paris, 1877.

Lingard, John—Belloc, Hilaire, *A History of England,* 11 vols., New York, 1912–1915.

Loening, Edgar, *Geschichte des deutschen Kirchenrechts,* 2 vols., Strassburg, 1878.

Mamachi, Tomaso, *Del Diritto Libero della Chiesa di Acquistare e di Possedere Beni Temporali,* 5 vols., 1769–1770, no place.

Mann, Horace K., *The Lives of the Popes in the Middle Ages,* 18 vols., St. Louis: B. Herder Book Co., 1902–1932.

Meurer, Christian, *Der Begriff und Eigenthuemer der heiligen Sachen,* 2 vols., Duesseldorf, no date.

Michaud, J., *Biographie Universelle,* 45 vols., Paris-Leipzig, 1854–1865.

Michiels, Gommarus, *Principia Generalia de Personis in Ecclesia,* Lublin: Universitas Catholica, 1932.

Migne, Jacques Paul, *Patrologiae Cursus Completus, Series Graeca,* 161 vols., Parisiis, 1856–1866.

———, *Patrologiae Cursus Completus, Series Latina,* 221 vols., Parisiis, 1844–1864.

Moroni, Gaetano, *Dizionario di Erudizione Storico-Ecclesiastica,* 109 vols., Venezia, 1840–1879.

Moulart, Ferdinand J., *L'Eglise et L'Etat,* 4 ed., Louvain-Paris, 1895.

Ottaviani, Alaphridus, *Institutiones Iuris Publici Ecclesiastici,* 2 vols., Typis Polyglottis Vaticanis, 1935–1936.

Pallavicino, Sforza, *Istoria del Concilio di Trento,* 3 vols., Napoli, 1853.

Pastor, Ludwig von, *History of the Popes,* 29 vols., St. Louis: B. Herder Book Co., 1906–1938.

Phillips, G., *Droit Ecclesiastique,* 3 vols., Paris, 1855.

Pirhing, Ernricus, *Ius Canonicum,* 5 vols., Dilingae, 1728.

Pistocchi, Marius, *De Bonis Ecclesiae Temporalibus,* Taurini: Marietti, 1932.

Poschinger, H. von, *Das Eigenthum am Kirchenvermoegen,* Muenchen, 1871.

Poulet, Charles, *A History of the Catholic Church,* 2 vols., St. Louis: B. Herder Book Co., 1934–1935.

Reiffenstuel, Anacletus, *Ius Canonicum Universum,* 5 vols., Parisiis, 1864–1882.

Rossi, Giovanni B. de, *Roma Sotteranea Cristiana,* 3 vols., Roma, 1864–1877.

Saegmueller, J. B., *Lehrbuch des katholischen Kirchenrechts,* Freiburg im Breisgau, 1900.

Satolli, Franciscus, *De Iure Publico Ecclesiastico Disceptationes,* Romae, 1891.

Schenkl, Maurus, *Institutiones Iuris Ecclesiastici Communis,* 2 vols., Landishuti, 1830.

Scheys, Carolus, *De Iure Ecclesiae Acquirendi et Possidendi Bona Temporalia,* Louvain, 1892.

Schmalzgrueber, Franciscus, *Ius Ecclesiasticum Universum,* 12 vols., Romae, 1843–1845.

Schroeder, H. J., *Disciplinary Decrees of the General Council,* St. Louis: B. Herder Book Co., 1937.

Schultes, Reginaldo Maria—Prantner, Edmundus, *De Ecclesia Catholica,* Parisiis: P. Lethielleux, 1931.

Sebastianelli, Gulielmus, *Praelectiones Iuris Canonici,* 2 ed., Romae, 1905.

Soglia, Ioannes, *Institutiones Iuris Publici Ecclesiastici,* 5 ed., Paris, n.d.

Stevenson, Joseph, *The Truth About John Wyclif,* London, 1885.

Taparelli, Luigi, *Saggio Teoretico di Dritto Naturale,* 2 vols., Roma, 1855.

Tarquini, Camillus, *Iuris Ecclesiastici Publici Institutiones,* 4 ed., Romae, 1875.

Thomas Aquinas, *De Regimine Principum,* translated into English by Gerald B. Phelan, Ph.D., and published under the title *On the Governance of Rulers,* New York: Sheed and Ward, 1938.

Thomassinus, Ludovicus, *Vetus et Nova Ecclesiae Disciplina,* 3 vols., Parisiis, 1688.

Tillmann, Fritz, *Das Johannesevangelium,* Bonn: Verlag von Peter Hanstein, 1922.

Tilloy, M., *Traité de Droit Canonique,* 2 vols., Paris, 1895.

Tocco, Felice, *L'Eresia nel Medio Evo,* Firenze, 1884.

Trevelyan, George M., *England in the Age of Wycliffe,* London, 1929.

Vacant, A—Mangenot, E., *Dictionnaire de Théologie Catholique,* 13 vols., Paris, 1903–1927.

Vermeersch, Arthurus—Creusen, Ioseph, *Epitome Iuris Canonici,* 3 vols., vol. I, 6 ed., Mechlinae: H. Dessain, 1937; vols. II and III, 5 ed., 1934–1936.

Vogt, Joseph, *Das kirchliche Vermoegensrecht,* Coeln, 1910.

Vromant, G., *De Bonis Ecclesiae Temporalibus,* Louvain: Desbarax, 1927.

Wenner, Joseph, *Kirchliches Vermoegensrecht,* Paderborn: Verlag Ferdinand Schoeningh, 1936.

Wernz, Franciscus, *Ius Decretalium,* vol. III, Romae, 1908.

Wernz, F.—Vidal, P., *Ius Canonicum,* vol. IV, Romae: Apud Aedes Universitatis Gregorianae, 1935.

Wrightington, Sydney R., *The Law of Unincorporated Associations,* Boston, 1916.

Zaccaria, F. A., *Anti-Febronius,* 5 vols., Bruxelles, 1829.

Zapelena, Timotheus, *De Ecclesia Christi,* 2 vols., Romae: Apud Aedes Universitatis Gregorianae, 1940.

Zollmann, Carl, *American Church Law,* St. Paul: West Publishing Co., 1933.

( ), *Confutazione degli Errori e Calunnie contro La Chiesa e La Sovranità,* 2 vols., 1794, no place.

( ), *De Finibus Utriusque Potestatis,* Lugani-Ratisbonae, 1781.

Articles

Couly, Aug., "Les Biens Temporels de L'Église,"—*Le Canoniste Contemporain,* XLIII (1920), 296–303; 392–399; 482–494.

Didier, Noel, "Les Origines du Droit Souverain d'amortissement dans le Comte de Hainaut,"—*Revue d'Historie Ecclésiastique,* XXXIV (1938), 487–503.

Grashof, Otto, "Die Gesetzgebung der roemischen Kaiser ueber die Gueter und Immunitaeten der Kirche und des Klerus nebst deren Motiven und Principien,"—*AKKR,* XXXVI (1876), 3–51.

———, "Die Gesetze der roemischen Kaiser ueber die Immunitaeten der Kirche hinsichtlich ihres Vermoegens,"—*AKKR,* XXXVI (1876), 321–335.

Hirschel, Dr., "Das Eigenthum am katholischen Kirchengute,"—*AKKR,* XXXIV (1875), 32–89; 259–355.

———, "Die Ansprueche der "Altkatholiken" auf Ueberlassung von Kirchen und Kirchengut,"—*AKKR,* XXXV (1876), 38–66.

———, "Sind bischoefliche Ordinariate erbfaehig?"—*AKKR,* XXVII (1872), 1–42.

Loehr, Josef, "Ueber die Natur der Rechte, die den Pfarrern und Glaeubigen waehrend des franzoesischen Trennungsgesetzes an den Kirchen zustehen," —*AKKR,* XCIV (1914), 577–604.

Maas, Heinrich, "Ueber das Rechtssubject, die Vertretung, Verwaltung und Verwendung des Kirchen-, Schul-, und Stiftungsvermoegens, mit besonderer Ruecksicht auf die Erzbischoefliche Verwaltungs-Instruction fur Hohenzollern,"—*AKKR,* IV (1859), 583–604, 644–704; V (1860), 3–35.

Mueller, Joseph, "Il concetto della Chiesa come "Societas Perfecta" in S. Tommaso d'Aquino e l'idea moderna della sovranità,"—*Rivista Internazionale di Scienze Sociali,* XCVII (1923), 193–204, 301–308.

Roberti, F., "Le associazioni funerarie cristiane e la proprietà ecclesiastica nei primi tre secoli,"—*Pubblicazioni della Università Cattolica del S. Cuore.* Serie settima—Scienze giuridiche, 1928.

Schmitz, Hermann, "Die Eigentumsfrage am Kirchenvermoegen und die neuere staatliche Gesetzgebung,"—*AKKR,* LXI (1889), 255–284.

Periodicals

Archiv fuer katholisches Kirchenrecht, Innsbruck, 1857–1861; Mainz, 1862—

Le Canoniste Contemporain, Paris, 1878—1926.

Pubblicazioni della Università Cattolica del S. Cuore. Serie settima—Scienze giuridiche, Milano, 1922—

Revue d'Histoire Ecclésiastique, Louvain, 1900—

Rivista Internazionale di Scienze Sociali e Discipline Ausiliarie, Roma, 1893—

ABBREVIATIONS

AAS—Acta Apostolicae Sedis.
AKKR—Archiv fuer katholisches Kirchenrecht.
Art.—Article.
ASS—Acta Sanctae Sedis.
Bull. Rom.—Bullarium Romanum.
C—Codex (Justinianus).
Can.—Canon.
Cap.—Caput.
Cc.—Canones.
Ch.—Chapitre.
Coll. Lac.—Acta et Decreta Sacrorum Conciliorum Recentiorum. Collectio Lacensis.
C. Th.—Codex Theodosianus.
D—Digesta (Justiniana).
Denz.—Enchiridion Symbolorum et Definitionum.
Fontes—Codicis Iuris Canonici Fontes cura . . . Gasparri editi.
Harduin—*Acta Conciliorum etc.*
I—Institutiones (Justinianae).
Liv.—Livre.
Mansi—*Sacrorum Conciliorum . . . Collectio.*
MPG—Migne, *Patrologia Graeca.*
MPL—Migne, *Patrologia Latina.*
N—Novellae (Justinianae).

BIOGRAPHICAL NOTE

JOHN ALOYSIUS GOODWINE was born in New York City on July 13, 1913. He received his primary education at the parochial school of St. Joseph of the Holy Family, New York City. His high school and college studies were made in St. Joseph's Seminary and College, New York and Yonkers, from which institution he received the degree of Bachelor of Arts in 1934. In October, 1934, he was appointed to the North American College, Rome, Italy, to make his theological studies at the Pontifical Gregorian University, where he received the Baccalaureate in Theology in 1936 and the Licentiate in Theology in 1938. He was ordained on July 25, 1937. In November, 1938, he entered the Canon Law School at the Gregorian University, Rome, receiving the Baccalaureate in Canon Law the following July. In September, 1939, because of political conditions in Europe, he was transferred to the Canon Law School at the Catholic University of America, Washington, D. C., where he received the Licentiate in Canon Law in June, 1940.

INDEX

CANON LAW STUDIES

1. Freriks, Rev. Celestine A., C.PP.S., J.C.D., Religious Congregations in Their External Relations, 121 pp., 1916.
2. Galliher, Rev. Daniel M., O.P., J.C.D., Canonical Elections, 117 pp., 1917.
3. Borkowski, Rev. Aurelius L., O.F.M., J.C.D., De Confraternitatibus Ecclesiasticis, 136 pp., 1918.
4. Castillo, Rev. Cayo, J.C.D., Disertacion Historico-Canonica sobre la Potestad del Cabildo en Sede Vacante o Impedida del Vicario Capitular, 99 pp., 1919 (1918).
5. Kubelbeck, Rev. William J., S.T.B., J.C.D., The Sacred Penitentiaria and Its Relation to Faculties of Ordinaries and Priests, 129 pp., 1918.
6. Petrovits, Rev. Joseph, J.C., S.T.D., J.C.D., The New Church Law on Matrimony, X–461 pp., 1919.
7. Hickey, Rev. John J., S.T.B., J.C.D., Irregularities and Simple Impediments in the New Code of Canon Law, 100 pp., 1920.
8. Klekotka, Rev. Peter J., S.T.B., J.C.D., Diocesan Consultors, 179 pp., 1920.
9. Wanenmacher, Rev. Francis, J.C.D., The Evidence in Ecclesiastical Procedure Affecting the Marriage Bond, 1920 (Printed 1935).
10. Golden, Rev. Henry Francis, J.C.D., Parochial Benefices in the New Code, IV–119 pp., 1921 (Printed 1925).
11. Koudelka, Rev. Charles J., J.C.D., Pastors, Their Rights and Duties According to the New Code of Canon Law, 211 pp., 1921.
12. Melo, Rev. Antonius, O.F.M., J.C.D., De Exemptione Regularium, X–188 pp., 1921.
13. Schaaf, Rev. Valentine Theodore, O.F.M., S.T.B., J.C.D., The Cloister, X–180 pp., 1921.
14. Burke, Rev. Thomas Joseph, S.T.D., J.C.D., Competence in Ecclesiastical Tribunals, IV–117 pp., 1922.
15. Leech, Rev. George Leo, J.C.D., A Comparative Study of the Constitution "Apostolicae Sedis" and the "Codex Juris Canonici," 179 pp., 1922.
16. Motry, Rev. Hubert Louis, S.T.D., J.C.D., Diocesan Faculties According to the Code of Canon Law, II–167 pp., 1922.
17. Murphy, Rev. George Lawrence, J.C.D., Delinquencies and Penalties in the Administration and the Reception of the Sacraments, IV–121 pp., 1923.
18. O'Reilly, Rev. John Anthony, S.T.B., J.C.D., Ecclesiastical Sepulture in the New Code of Canon Law, II–129 pp., 1923.
19. Michalicka, Rev. Wenceslas Cyrill, O.S.B., J.C.D., Judicial Procedure in Dismissal of Clerical Exempt Religious, 107 pp. 1923.
20. Dargin, Rev. Edward Vincent, S.T.B., J.C.D., Reserved Cases According to the Code of Canon Law, IV–103 pp., 1924.
21. Godfrey, Rev. John A., S.T.B., J.C.D., The Right of Patronage According to the Code of Canon Law, 153 pp., 1924.

22. Hagedorn, Rev. Francis Edward, J.C.D., General Legislation on Indulgences, II–154 pp., 1924.
23. King, Rev. James Ignatius, J.C.D., The Administration of the Sacraments to Dying Non-Catholics, V–141 pp., 1924.
24. Winslow, Rev. Francis Joseph, M.M., J.C.D., Vicars and Prefects Apostolic, IV–149 pp., 1924.
25. Correa, Rev. Jose Servelion, S.T.L., J.C.D., La Potestad Legislativa de la Iglesia Catolica, IV–127 pp., 1925.
26. Dugan, Rev. Henry Francis, A.M., J.C.D., The Judiciary Department of the Diocesan Curia, 87 pp., 1925.
27. Keller, Rev. Charles Frederick, S.T.B., J.C.D., Mass Stipends, 167 pp., 1925.
28. Paschang, Rev. John Linus, J.C.D., The Sacramentals According to the Code of Canon Law, 129 pp., 1925.
29. Pointek, Rev. Cyrillus, O.F.M., S.T.B., J.C.D., De Indulto Exclaustrationis necnon Saecularizationis, XIII–289 pp., 1925.
30. Kearney, Rev. Richard Joseph, S.T.B., J.C.D., Sponsors at Baptism According to the Code of Canon Law, IV–127 pp., 1925.
31. Bartlett, Rev. Chester Joseph, A.M., LL.B., J.C.D., The Tenure of Parochial Property in the United States of America, V–108 pp., 1926.
32. Kilker, Rev. Adrian Jerome, J.C.D., Extreme Unction, V–425 pp., 1926.
33. McCormick, Rev. Robert Emmett, J.C.D., Confessors of Religious, VIII–266 pp., 1926.
34. Miller, Rev. Newton Thomas, J.C.D., Founded Masses According to the Code of Canon Law, VII–93 pp., 1926.
35. Roelker, Rev. Edward G., S.T.D., J.C.D., Principles of Privilege According to the Code of Canon Law, XI–166 pp., 1926.
36. Bakalarczyk, Rev. Richardus, M.I.C., J.U.D., De Novitiatu, VIII–208 pp., 1927.
37. Pizzuti, Rev. Lawrence, O.F.M., J.U.L., De Parochis Religiosis, 1927. (Not Printed.)
38. Bliley, Rev. Nicholas Martin, O.S.B., J.C.D., Altars According to the Code of Canon Law, XIX–132 pp., 1927.
39. Brown, Mr. Brendan Francis, A.B., LL.M., J.U.D., The Canonical Juristic Personality with Special Reference to its Status in the United States of America, V–212 pp., 1927.
40. Cavanaugh, Rev. William Thomas, C.P., J.U.D., The Reservation of the Blessed Sacrament, VIII–101 pp., 1927.
41. Doheny, Rev. William J., C.S.C., A.B., J.U.D., Church Property: Modes of Acquisition, X–118 pp., 1927.
42. Feldhaus, Rev. Aloysius H., C.PP.S., J.C.D., Oratories, IX–141 pp., 1927.
43. Kelly, Rev. James Patrick, A.B., J.C.D., The Jurisdiction of the Simple Confessor, X–208 pp., 1927.
44. Neuberger, Rev. Nicholas J., J.C.D., Canon 6 or the Relation of the

Codex Juris Canonici to the Preceding Legislation, V–95 pp., 1927.

45. O'Keefe, Rev. Gerald Michael, J.C.D., Matrimonial Dispensations, Powers of Bishops, Priests, and Confessors, VIII–232 pp., 1927.
46. Quigley, Rev. Joseph A. M., A.B., J.C.D., Condemned Societies, 139 pp., 1927.
47. Zaplotnik, Rev. Johannes Leo, J.C.D., De Vicariis Foraneis, X–142 pp., 1927.
48. Duskie, Rev. John Aloysius, A.B., J.C.D., The Canonical Status of the Orientals in the United States, VIII–196 pp., 1928.
49. Hyland, Rev. Francis Edward, J.C.D., Excommunication, Its Nature, Historical Development and Effects, VIII–181 pp., 1928.
50. Reinmann, Rev. Gerald Joseph, O.M.C., J.C.D., The Third Order Secular of Saint Francis, 201 pp., 1928.
51. Schenk, Rev. Francis J., J.C.D., The Matrimonial Impediments of Mixed Religion and Disparity of Cult, XVI–318 pp., 1929.
52. Coady, Rev. John Joseph, S.T.D., J.U.D., A.M., The Appointment of Pastors, VIII–150 pp., 1929.
53. Kay, Rev. Thomas Henry, J.C.D., Competence in Matrimonial Procedure, VIII–164 pp., 1929.
54. Turner, Rev. Sidney Joseph, C.P., J.U.D., The Vow of Poverty, XLIX–217 pp., 1929.
55. Kearney, Rev. Raymond A., A.B., S.T.D., J.C.D., The Principles of Delegation, VII–149 pp., 1929.
56. Conran, Rev. Edward James, A.B., J.C.D., The Interdict, V–163 pp., 1930.
57. O'Neill, Rev. William H., J.C.D., Papal Rescripts of Favor, VII–218 pp., 1930.
58. Bastnagel, Rev. Clement Vincent, J.U.D., The Appointment of Parochial Adjutants and Assistants, XV–257 pp., 1940.
59. Ferry, Rev. William A., A.B., J.C.D., Stole Fees, V–136 pp., 1930.
60. Costello, Rev. John Michael, A.B., J.C.D., Domicile and Quasi-Domicile, VII–201 pp., 1930.
61. Kremer, Rev. Michael Nicholas, A.B., S.T.B., J.C.D., Church Support in the United States, VI–136 pp., 1930.
62. Angulo, Rev. Luis, C.M., J.C.D., Legislation de la Iglesia sobre la intencion en la application de la Santa Misa, VII–104 pp., 1931.
63. Frey, Rev. Wolfgang Norbert, O.S.B., A.B., J.C.D., The Act of Religious Profession, VIII–174 pp., 1931.
64. Roberts, Rev. James Brendan, A.B., J.C.D., The Banns of Marriage, XIV–140 pp., 1931.
65. Ryder, Rev. Raymond Aloysius, A.B., J.C.D., Simony, IX–151 pp., 1931.
66. Campagna, Rev. Angelo, Ph.D., J.U.D., Il Vicario Generale del Vescovo, VII–205 pp., 1931.
67. Cox, Rev. Joseph Godfrey, A.B., J.C.D., The Administration of Seminaries, VI–124 pp., 1931.

68. GREGORY, REV. DONALD J., J.U.D., The Pauline Privilege, XV–165 pp., 1931.
69. DONOHUE, REV. JOHN F., J.C.D., The Impediment of Crime, VII–110 pp., 1931.
70. DOOLEY, REV. EUGENE A., O.M.I., J.C.D., Church Law on Sacred Relics, IX–143 pp., 1931.
71. ORTH, REV. CLEMENT RAYMOND, O.M.C., J.C.D., The Approbation of Religious Institutes, 171 pp., 1931.
72. PERNICONE, REV. JOSEPH M., A.B., J.C.D., The Ecclesiastical Prohibition of Books, XII–267 pp., 1932.
73. CLINTON, REV. CONNELL, A.B., J.C.D., The Paschal Precept, IX–108 pp., 1932.
74. DONNELLY, REV. FRANCIS B., A.M., S.T.L., J.C.D., The Diocesan Synod, VIII–125 pp., 1932.
75. TORRENTE, REV. CAMILO, C.M.F., J.C.D., Las Processiones Sagradas, V–145 pp., 1932.
76. MURPHY, REV. EDWIN J., C.PP.S., J.C.D., Suspension Ex Informata Conscientia, XI–122 pp., 1932.
77. MACKENZIE, REV. ERIC F., A.M., S.T.L., J.C.D., The Delicit of Heresy in Its Commission, Penalization, Absolution, VII–124 pp., 1932.
78. LYONS, REV. AVITUS E., S.T.B., J.C.D., The Collegiate Tribunal of First Instance, XI–147 pp., 1932.
79. CONNOLLY, REV. THOMAS A., J.C.D., Appeals, XI–195 pp., 1932.
80. SANGMEISTER, REV. JOSEPH V., A.B., J.C.D., Force and Fear as Precluding Matrimonial Consent, V–211 pp., 1932.
81. JAEGER, REV. LEO A., A.B., J.C.D., The Administration of Vacant and Quasi-Vacant Episcopal Sees in the United States, IX–229 pp., 1932.
82. RIMLINGER, REV. HERBERT T., J.C.D., Error Invalidating Matrimonial Consent, VII–79 pp., 1932.
83. BARRETT, REV. JOHN D. M., S.S., J.C.D., A Comparative Study of the Third Plenary Council of Baltimore and the Code, IX–221 pp., 1932.
84. CARBERRY, REV. JOHN J., PH.D., S.T.D., J.C.D., The Juridical Form of Marriage, X–177 pp., 1934.
85. DOLAN, REV. JOHN L., A.B., J.C.D., The Defensor Vinculi, XII–157 pp., 1934.
86. HANNAN, REV. JEROME D., A.M., S.T.D., LL.B., J.C.D., The Canon Law of Wills, IX–517 pp., 1934.
87. LEMIEUX, REV. DELISE A., A.M., J.C.D., The Sentence in Ecclesiastical Procedure, IX–131 pp., 1934.
88. O'ROURKE, REV. JAMES J., A.B., J.C.D., Parish Registers, VII–109 pp., 1934.
89. TIMLIN, REV. BARTHOLOMEW, O.F.M., A.M., J.C.D., Conditional Matrimonial Consent, X–381 pp., 1934.
90. WAHL, REV. FRANCIS X., A.B., J.C.D., The Matrimonial Impediments of Consanguinity and Affinity, VI–125 pp., 1934.
91. WHITE, REV. ROBERT J., A.B., LL.B., S.T.B., J.C.D., Canonical Ante-Nuptial Promises and the Civil Law, VI–152 pp., 1934.

92. HERRERA, REV. ANTONIO PARRA, O.C.D., J.C.D., Legislacion Ecclesiastica sobra el Ayuno y la Abstinencia, XI–191 pp., 1935.
93. KENNEDY, REV. EDWIN J., J.C.D., The Special Matrimonial Process in Cases of Evident Nullity, X–165 pp., 1935.
94. MANNING, REV. JOHN J., A.B., J.C.D., Presumption of Law in Matrimonial Procedure, XI–111 pp., 1935.
95. MOEDER, REV. JOHN M., J.C.D., The Proper Bishop for Ordination and Dimissorial Letters, VII–135 pp., 1935.
96. O'MARA, REV. WILLIAM A., A.B., J.C.D., Canonical Causes for Matrimonial Dispensations, IX–155 pp., 1935.
97. REILLY, REV. PETER, J.C.D., Residence of Pastors, IX–81 pp., 1935.
98. SMITH, REV. MARINER T., O.P., S.T.Lr., J.C.D., The Penal Law for Religious, VII–169 pp., 1935.
99. WHALEN, REV. DONALD W., A.M., J.C.D., The Value of Testimonial Evidence in Matrimonial Procedure, XIII–297 pp., 1935.
100. CLEARY, REV. JOSEPH F., J.C.D., Canonical Limitations on the Alienation of Church Property, VIII–141 pp., 1936.
101. GLYNN, REV. JOHN C., J.C.D., The Promoter of Justice, XX–337 pp., 1936.
102. BRENNAN, REV. JAMES H., S.S., M.A., S.T.B., J.C.D., The Simple Convalidation of Marriage, VI–135 pp., 1937.
103. BRUNINI, REV. JOSEPH BERNARD, J.C.D., The Clerical Obligations of Canons 139 and 142, X–121 pp., 1937.
104. CONNOR, REV. MAURICE, A.B., J.C.D., The Administrative Removal of Pastors, VIII–159 pp., 1937.
105. GUILFOYLE, REV. MERLIN JOSEPH, J.C.D., Custom, XI–144 pp., 1937.
106. HUGHES, REV. JAMES AUSTIN, A.B., A.M., J.C.D., Witnesses in Criminal Trials of Clerics, IX–140 pp., 1937.
107. JANSEN, REV. RAYMOND J., A.B., S.T.L., J.C.D., Canonical Provisions for Catechetical Instruction, VII–153 pp., 1937.
108. KEALY, REV. JOHN JAMES, A.B., J.C.D., The Introductory Libellus in Church Court Procedure, XI–121 pp., 1937.
109. MCMANUS, REV. JAMES EDWARD, C.SS.R., J.C.D., The Administration of Temporal Goods in Religious Institutes, XVI–196 pp., 1937.
110. MORIARTY, REV. EUGENE JAMES, J.C.D., Oaths in Ecclesiastical Courts, X–115 pp., 1937.
111. RAINER, REV. ELIGIUS GEORGE, C.SS.R., J.C.D., Suspension of Clerics, XVII–249 pp., 1937.
112. REILLY, REV. THOMAS F., C.SS.R., J.C.D., Visitation of Religious, VI–195 pp., 1938.
113. MORIARITY, REV. FRANCIS E., C.SS.R., J.C.D., The Extraordinary Absolution from Censures, XV–334 pp., 1938.
114. CONNOLLY, REV. NICHOLAS P., J.C.D., The Canonical Erection of Parishes, X–132 pp., 1938.
115. DONOVAN, REV. JAMES JOSEPH, J.C.D., The Pastor's Obligation in Prenuptial Investigation, XII–322 pp., 1938.

116. HARRIGAN, REV. ROBERT J., M.A., S.T.B., J.C.D., The Radical Sanation of Invalid Marriages, VIII–208 pp., 1938.
117. BOFFA, REV. CONRAD HUMBERT, J.C.D., Canonical Provisions for Catholic Schools, VII–211 pp., 1939.
118. PARSONS, REV. ANSCAR JOHN, O.M.Cap., J.C.D., Canonical Elections, XII–236 pp., 1939.
119. REILLY, REV. EDWARD MICHAEL, A.B., J.C.D., The General Norms of Dispensation, XII–156 pp., 1939.
120. RYAN, REV. GERALD ALOYSIUS, A.B., J.C.D., Principles of Episcopal Jurisdiction, XII–172 pp., 1939.
121. BURTON, REV. FRANCIS JAMES, C.S.C., A.B., J.C.D., A Commentary on Canon 1125, X–222 pp., 1940.
122. MIASKIEWICZ, REV. FRANCIS SIGISMUND, J.C.D., Supplied Jurisdiction According to Canon 209, XII–340 pp., 1940.
123. RICE, REV. PATRICK WILLIAM, A.B., J.C.D., Proof of Death in Prenuptial Investigation, VIII–156 pp., 1940.
124. ANGLIN, REV. THOMAS FRANCIS, M.S., J.C.L., The Eucharistic Fast.
125. COLEMAN, REV. JOHN JEROME, J.C.L., The Minister of Confirmation.
126. DOWNS, REV. JOHN EMMANUEL, A.B., J.C.L., The Concept of Clerical Immunity.
127. ESSWEIN, REV. ANTHONY ALBERT, J.C.L., Extrajudicial Penal Powers of Ecclesiastical Superiors.
128. FARRELL, REV. BENJAMIN FRANCIS, M.A., S.T.L., J.C.L., The Rights and Duties of the Local Ordinary Regarding Congregations of Women Religious of Pontifical Approval.
129. FEENEY, REV. THOMAS JOHN, A.B., S.T.L., J.C.L., Restitutio in Integrum.
130. FINDLAY, REV. STEPHEN WILLIAM, O.S.B., A.B., J.C.L., Canonical Norms Governing the Deposition and Degradation of Clerics.
131. GOODWINE, REV. JOHN, A.B., S.T.L., J.C.L., The Right of the Church to Acquire Property.
132. HESTON, REV. EDWARD LOUIS, C.S.C., PH.D., S.T.D., J.C.L., The Alienation of Church Property in the United States.
133. HOGAN, REV. JAMES JOHN, S.T.L., J.C.L., Judicial Advocates and Procurators.
134. KEALY, REV. THOMAS M., A.B., LITT.B., J.C.L., Dowry of Women Religious.
135. KEENE, REV. MICHAEL JAMES, O.S.B., J.C.L., Religious Ordinaries and Canon 198.
136. KERIN, REV. CHARLES A., S.S., M.A., S.T.B., J.C.L., The Privation of Christian Burial.
137. LOUIS, REV. WILLIAM FRANCIS, M.A., J.C.L., Diocesan Archives.
138. McDEVITT, REV. GILBERT JOSEPH, A.B., J.C.L., Legitimacy and Legitimation.
139. McDONOUGH, REV. THOMAS JOSEPH, A.B., J.C.L., Apostolic Administrators.

140. MEIER, REV. CARL ANTHONY, A.B., J.C.L., Penal Administrative Procedure Against Negligent Pastors.
141. SCHMIDT, REV. JOHN ROGG, A.B., J.C.L., The Principles of Authentic Interpretation in Canon 17 of the Code of Canon Law.
142. SLAFKOSKY, REV. ANDREW LEONARD, A.B., J.C.L., The Canonical Episcopal Visitation of the Diocese.
143. SWOBODA, REV. INNOCENT ROBERT, O.F.M., J.C.L., Ignorance in Relation to the Imputability of Delicts.
144. DUBÉ, REV. ARTHUR JOSEPH, A.B., J.C.L., The General Principles for the Reckoning of Time in Canon Law.
145. McBRIDE, REV. JAMES T., A.B., J.C.L., Incardination and Excardination of Seculars.

www.ingramcontent.com/pod-product-compliance
Lightning Source LLC
LaVergne TN
LVHW050205080826
844660LV00012B/359

* 9 7 8 0 8 1 3 2 2 3 2 0 9 *